COLLEGE
PRESENTATION

Bridge
Better
Communication

英語プレゼンテーション教材開発研究チーム

Materials Development Team on Presentations in English

KINSEIDO

Kinseido Publishing Co., Ltd.

3-21 Kanda Jimbo-cho, Chiyoda-ku,

Tokyo 101-0051, Japan

First published 2020 by Kinseido Publishing Co., Ltd.

Cover design   Nampoosha Co., Ltd.

 音声ファイル無料ダウンロード

http://www.kinsei-do.co.jp/download/4099

この教科書で DL 00 の表示がある箇所の音声は、上記 URL または QR コードにて無料でダウンロードできます。自習用音声としてご活用ください。

▶ PC からのダウンロードをお勧めします。スマートフォンなどでダウンロードされる場合は、ダウンロード前に「**解凍アプリ**」を**インストール**してください。
▶ URL は、**検索ボックスではなくアドレスバー (URL 表示欄)** に入力してください。
▶ お使いのネットワーク環境によっては、ダウンロードできない場合があります。

CD 00 ▶ 左記の表示がある箇所の音声は、教室用 CD (Class Audio CD) に収録されています。

は　じ　め　に

　本テキストは、大学生にとって興味深いテーマのアカデミック・プレゼンテーション（人文・社会・自然科学をカバーした全15本のビデオ）の視聴・内容理解を通して、英語プレゼンテーションに必要な論理的展開方法と、英語プレゼンテーションでよく使われる英語表現を学ぶことを目的としています。

　本テキストの構成は以下のようになっています。各章で、まず、内容理解のためのキーワードの意味をチェックします。その後で、プレゼンテーションのビデオ全体を通して観て、概要の把握をします。次に、パート毎にビデオを見て詳しい内容を理解します。その後、プレゼンテーションや論理的な英文でよく使われる英語表現の整序問題を行い、重要表現を覚えます。それに続き、プレゼンテーションで使われているスライドを参考に、プレゼンテーション全体の流れを意識しながら、英文要約の空所補充問題を行います。最後に、重要表現を音声で聞き、ディクテーションで表現を確認した後で、本テキスト独自のシャドーイングを応用した学習活動を行います。「テキストを見ながら」「字幕付き」「ヒント付き」「字幕なし」という4種類の方法でビデオを観ながら、飽きずに段階的に練習できるようになっています。お手本のプレゼンテーションに合わせて、同じ速さ・イントネーション・アクセントで発話するという学習活動です。このように、実際に声に出して発話してみることで、よく使われる表現を、イントネーションやアクセントも含めて自然に覚えられるようになっています。

　本テキストのもとになったものは、名古屋大学で英語のプレゼンテーションを学ぶ授業の課外自主学習用として開発されたe-learning教材『eFACE』です。この教材は、教室で行われる授業とは独立して学べるようになっており、実際のプレゼンテーションの練習は教室で行い、その補助として論理的な構成のプレゼンテーションのお手本を見て理解し、そこで使われる基礎的な表現を課外で自主学習するというものです。本テキストは、そのコンテンツをもとに英語プレゼンテーションの基礎を教室の授業で学べるように加筆修正し、編集しなおしたものです。

本テキストは授業で使うことを想定して作られていますが、使い方によっては、テキストを事前に自習した上で、授業内では実際のプレゼンテーション活動を行うというアクティブラーニングを行うこともできます。実際のプレゼンテーション活動に役立てるように、各ユニットには「Presentation Tips」を掲載しています。また、巻末に「使用場面別　プレゼンテーションで役立つ表現 124」をまとめてありますので、こちらもプレゼンテーションの準備に是非活用ください。

　もととなった『eFACE』は名古屋大学の多くの先生方の協力を得て開発されました。ここに記して感謝の意を表します。また、金星堂の長島吉成氏には本テキストのシャドーイングを応用した学習活動部分のビデオ編集をはじめ学習活動の提案などで、平田英司氏には本テキストの出版について最初から最後までお世話をいただきました。記して感謝の意を表します。

英語プレゼンテーション教材開発研究チーム

杉浦正利　尾関修治　松原緑　小松雅宏　古泉隆　石田知美

CONTENTS

CONTENTS

プレゼンテーションとは
——観る前、行う前に知っておきたいこと

プレゼンテーションにおける三種類のパターン：内容・構造・表現

　プレゼンテーションは、自分の「考え」を相手にわかってもらうことです。では、どうしたら相手にわかってもらいやすくなるでしょうか。人は、パターンで理解します。プレゼンテーションでも、パターンを使うことが、わかりやすくするコツです。次の三つのパターンを意識しましょう。

①内容のパターン

　「内容のパターン」とは、話の内容をよく整理整頓しておくことです。どんな内容を盛り込むか、よく考えましょう。関係していれば何でも良いわけではありません。準備としてアイデアを練るときは思いつくままに書き出してみることで広がりが出ます（これをブレーンストーミングと言います）が、その後、何が重要かを考えて、大切なことだけに絞る必要があります。関係があっても重要でないことは「捨てる」必要があります。そして、どんな順番で話をするか、よく考えましょう。話の展開を考えるわけです。

時間順に話すのか、二つを対比して相違を説明するのか、原因と結果という因果関係を説明するのか、それとも、分類して説明するのかなど、どのような展開にするかを意識して、話す内容を並べてみましょう。

②構造のパターン

　二つ目の「構造のパターン」とは、英文のパラグラフの構造や、エッセイの文章構成法と同じように、文章に構造を持たせることです。「構造」とは、全体が複数の部分から成り立っていて、各部分には、それぞれ全体の中での役割があるということです。つまり、パラグラフが、トピック文と支持文とまとめ文で構成されていること、そして、複数のパラグラフからなるエッセイが、Introduction（序論）、Body（本論）、Conclusion（結論）から構成されていることです。プレゼンテーションの原稿も、同様に、構造を持たせる必要があります。プレゼンテーションも、基本的には、エッセイの構造と同じです。

Introduction	=	プレゼンテーションの導入では、何について、どのような順で話すかを説明する。最初に、いかに聴衆をひきつけるかがポイントになる。最近の話題や一般論で話し始めたり、聴衆に問いかけたりすると効果的。
Body	=	話す内容は、三つくらい（三段落）にまとめて話すとよい。それぞれ、何について話すか明確に示してから、具体的な内容を述べるようにする。意見や判断を述べるときは必ず根拠を示すようにすること。段落間はつなぎ言葉でつなげる。
Conclusion	=	最後に、これまで話してきたことを簡潔に「まとめ」る。起承転結の「結」ではないので注意。意見や主張は Body の部分ではっきりと詳しく述べておき、ここではそのポイントをまとめるだけにする。

③表現のパターン

　三つ目の「表現のパターン」とは、プレゼンテーションでよく使われる決まった表現、すなわち定型表現があるので、そうした定型表現を使うことです。定型表現には二種類あります。一つ目は、いわゆるつなぎ言葉といわれるもので、項目を挙げる First, Second, Lastly や、論理的結果を示す Therefore、そして対比を示す On the other hand などです。もう一種類は、つなぎ言葉のように話の流れを示すのではなく、As you can see here とか It seems that ... のように、話の内容（メッセージ）そのものではなく、話の内容をひとつ上のレベルで包み込むようにカバーして相手に伝えるために使われる表現です。

では、実際のプレゼンテーションを参考に、三つのパターンがどのように使われているかを観察してみましょう。

以下は、これから観るプレゼンテーションのスクリプトです。あとに続く 3 つの TASK の解答を、プレゼンテーションを観ながらスクリプトに書き込んでください。

online/video

Using Web Search Engines for Learning English

Good morning. Today, I will show you how to use familiar web search engines to find example sentences that are useful for learning English. Specifically, this will include phrase searches, site-specific searches and, finally, wildcard searches. Note that there may be some search engines with which these methods do not work. In such cases, try another search engine.

5　First, let's look at the "phrase search." Let's say that you wrote a self-introduction, and it included the sentence, "I am a sophomore college student." We can use a search engine to see if this particular construction is a common expression. Okay, so let's type the phrase in as-is. What happens? You get a lot of hits for it, don't you? If you look, though, there are irrelevant pages included in the results, aren't there? That's because when you search, the order in which the
10　words are typed is ignored. That spells trouble when you want to search for a specific English expression. So, what can we do? Try putting the phrase in double quotation marks. Now do the search again. This time, all you get should be pages that include the exact phrase you entered. You still have a lot of hits. So, does this mean the phrase is common? Wait just a second. There are pages from around the world on the Web, and you often don't know who authored them.
15　When searching for example English sentences, you only want to use reliable English websites, right?

So, let me introduce a method for specifying the sites to search. At the end of your search phrase, add "site:edu". By including "site:", you can specify which sites to search. If you put "edu" after "site:", the search will be limited to those sites that include "edu" in the top-level domain.
20　Most sites with domains ending in "edu" are educational institutions in the United States. For British universities, you can use "ac.uk". All right. So now that you have added "site:edu" to your search, you have a very low number of hits. What does that tell you? It's not always the case, but a low number of hits suggests that the phrase entered is not so common. Actually, the expression "I am a sophomore college student" is not natural, and you should look for another expression.

25　So, what's our next move? I suggest we try what is called a "wildcard search." If you use a wildcard indicated by an asterisk, you can perform a flexible phrase search to find various expressions. In a phrase search, the asterisk stands for any word or words in that place in the phrase. For example, type in "I am a sophomore" and then put an asterisk after the phrase. What happens now?　You should have gotten various expressions like "I am a sophomore at

3

such and such university" or "I am a sophomore majoring in such and such," depending on what search engine you use. The important point here is to always check the context of the expressions you find.

Okay, let's go over the main points again. Today, we have looked at how to use web search engines to find example sentences useful for learning English. There are just three things to keep in mind. First, to search for a particular phrase, put it in double quotation marks. Then, to specify the sites to search, add "site:" at the end. Finally, to perform a flexible phrase search, use an asterisk in the phrase. I think you can now make a brief self-introduction in English. Okay. Let's hear somebody. Yes, you go ahead, please. Okay, you are a sophomore at Nagoya University. Very good. And one more. Yes, you, please. Okay, you are a sophomore majoring in economics. Well done. Thank you. I guess that's it for today. Thank you for participating.

TASK 1
最初に、一度全体を通して見て、何について、どんなことが取り上げられているか、考えてみましょう。キーワードを○で囲みましょう。

TASK 2
次に、Introduction（序論）、Body（本論）、Conclusion（結論）という、文章構成を意識して、どの部分がどの役割を果たしているか、考えてみましょう。パラグラフごとに、文章構成の役割を記入してください。また、各パラグラフの構造がどうなっているか、分析してみましょう。

TASK 3
最後に、英語の表現に注目して、つなぎ言葉や、メッセージをカバーして伝える表現として、どのようなものが使われているか、チェックしてみましょう。定型表現に下線を引いてみましょう。

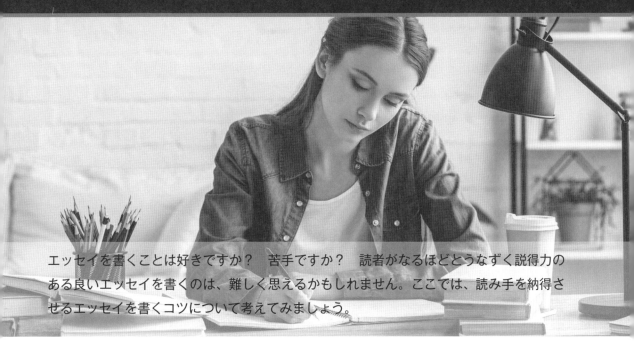

Unit 1

Argumentation in Essays

エッセイを書くことは好きですか？　苦手ですか？　読者がなるほどとうなずく説得力の
ある良いエッセイを書くのは、難しく思えるかもしれません。ここでは、読み手を納得さ
せるエッセイを書くコツについて考えてみましょう。

Keywords Check

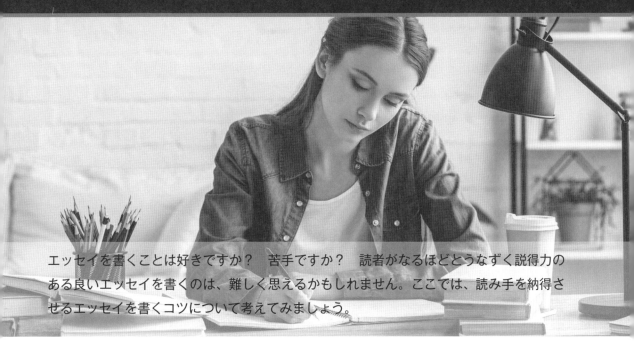

Choose the correct definition in Japanese for each word.
それぞれの単語の意味を選択肢から選びましょう。

online / audio

🎧 DL 02　◎ CD 1-02

1. argumentation 　　[　]　　　**2.** evidence 　　　[　]

3. applicable 　　　[　]　　　**4.** constitute 　　　[　]

5. persuasive 　　　[　]　　　**6.** logical 　　　　[　]

7. reading 　　　　[　]　　　**8.** barometer 　　　[　]

9. claim 　　　　　[　]　　　**10.** illustration 　　[　]

---

a. 論理的　**b.** 気圧計　**c.** 裏付け　**d.**（計器の）表示値・示度　**e.** 論証
f. 説得力のある　**g.** 適用可能な　**h.** 主張　**i.** 構成する　**j.** 説明

▶ Watch the Presentation (1st Viewing)

Watch the presentation and answer T(true) or F(false) for each of the following sentences.
プレゼンテーション映像を通しで観て、次の文が正しければ T を、そうでなければ F を選びましょう。

1. The main topic of this presentation is the relationship between reading and writing. 　　　　　　　　　　　　　　　　　　　　　　　　　　　 [T / F]

2. The claim of the argument needs to be persuasive. 　　　　　 [T / F]

3. The presentation mentions the importance of the topic sentence in a paragraph. 　　　　　　　　　　　　　　　　　　　　　　　　 [T / F]

4. The argument contains supporting reasons. 　　　　　　　　 [T / F]

▶ Focus for Better Understanding (2nd Viewing)

Watch three short parts of the presentation for a closer understanding and answer the questions.
次にプレゼンテーション映像をパートごとに観て、それぞれの問題に答えましょう。

Part I

DL 03　　CD 1-03

What is needed for a claim to be persuasive?

a. readiness

b. audience

c. reasons

d. experiences

Part II

DL 04　　CD 1-04

Why is the reading on the barometer a reliable reason?

a. You can check it with your own eyes.

b. There are many kinds of barometers.

c. The reading on the barometer drops quickly.

d. The mechanism of the barometer is simple.

Part III

Which statement is true of argumentation?

a. Collecting good evidence is a difficult task when preparing argumentation.

b. The reliability of the evidence has much to do with the persuasiveness of the argumentation.

c. Many people use graphic illustrations in their argumentation.

d. Methods of argumentation differ from one culture to another.

Useful Phrases

Choose appropriate words from the box to complete each sentence.

日本語に合うように下線部に入る語句を語群から組み合わせて選び、文を完成させましょう（語群では文頭に来る語も小文字で始めています）。

1.「これであなたは～に慣れるでしょう」

I hope that _____ the characteristics of an argument.

2.「簡単にいえば」

_____, whether or not an argument is persuasive depends on whether or not the reasons for the argument are reliable.

3.「信頼性があればあるほど」

_____ these are, the more persuasive the argument.

4.「あなたの主張を裏付けする」

Please work on using persuasive arguments to _____ when writing essays.

---

will / more / put / your claims / this / reliable / familiarize you /
with / support / the / simply

Summarize the Presentation

online audio

DL 06~10   CD 1-06 ~ CD 1-10

Read the summary of the presentation and fill in the blanks to complete the sentences for each slide.

スライドを参考に、空所に適語を入れプレゼンテーションの要約を完成させましょう。

1.

Argumentation in Essays

In today's (^{1}), I will clarify what generally constitutes an (^{2}) and then show what makes an argument (^{3}).

2.

Argument?

"My claim is A" is not enough.

The logical use of supporting reasons

If you just say, "My (^{4}) is A," it isn't persuasive. An argument is a statement in which you try to (^{5}) an (^{6}) of your claim by (^{7}) (   ) of supporting reasons.

3.

Cry of the rain god!?

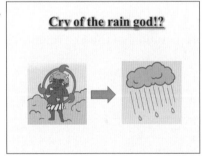

For example, what if someone made an argument like, "It's getting ready to (^{8}). I know that because when I hear the cry of the (^{9}) (   ), it rains soon after."

4.

Persuasive Argument

○ The reading on the barometer

You can check with your own eyes.

✗ Hearing the cry of the rain god

There is no way to verify it.

Whether or not an argument is (¹⁰   ) depends on whether or not the reasons for the argument are reliable. To make a strong argument, the (¹¹   ) must be backed up by sufficient (¹²   ).

5.

Conclusion

*An argument contains reasons and supporting evidence.

*Good reasons and evidence make claims more solid.

*The ability to use arguments is essential for writing essays.

The argument contains reasons and (¹³   ) (   ). By understanding the role of arguments, you can make more (¹⁴   ) (   ) in your own (¹⁵   ), and you will know where to look when following an argument in someone else's essay. The ability to use arguments is (¹⁶   ) (   )

writing essays and is also an important foundation for academic activities.

プレゼンテーション（オーディエンスと目的）

Presentation Tips

　プレゼンテーションは、自分が言いたいことを言うことではなく、コミュニケーションです。つまり、相手にわかってもらって初めて成り立つものです。相手といっても一人ではなく大勢です。しかし、大勢という集団に話しかけるのではありません。話すのは一人、オーディエンスは多数という「一対多」の関係ではなく、聞いてくれる聴衆の一人ひとりがあなたの話に耳を傾けています。つまり、「一対一」の関係がたくさんあるのです。一人ひとりにわかってもらおうという心がけで話しかけてください。

　相手にわかってもらうということは、裏返せば、相手がわかったと思うことです。相手が「なるほど、そうか、わかった」と思ってくれたら、そのプレゼンテーションは成功したといえます。では、何をどう話すとよいのでしょうか。そのコツは、相手が知りたいことを相手がわかるように話すことです。「相手は何を知りたいのかな？」「どうやったらわかってくれるのかな？」と考えてみてください。それが、上手なプレゼンテーションをする秘訣です。各ユニットにある Presentation Tips では効果的なプレゼンテーションにつながる具体的な秘訣が紹介されています。

▶️ Dictation and Shadowing

online / video

Step 1 Listen and complete the sentences with suitable words. 🎧 DL 11 💿 CD 1-11
音声を聞いて、空所に適切な語を入れましょう。

1. _____ _____ _____, you have to have argumentation in

an essay.

2. In today's presentation, _____ _____ _____ what

generally constitutes an argument.

3. Please _____ _____ _____ _____ this slide.

4. _____ _____ _____ a graphic illustration of the

argument.

Step 2 Following the video directions, practice A to D.
映像の指示にしたがって、A～D の練習をしましょう。

A Say the sentences aloud for Step 1 with audio and text.
Step 1 の文を映像（テキストと音声）と一緒に発声しましょう。

B Say them aloud with the excerpted videos (with subtitles).
Step 1 の文を映像（字幕）と一緒に発声しましょう。

C Say them aloud with the excerpted videos (with only
partially completed subtitles).
Step 1 の文を映像（一部以外はすべて空白の字幕）と
一緒に発声しましょう。

D Say them aloud with the excerpted videos (no subtitles).
Step 1 の文を映像（字幕なし）と一緒に発声しましょう。

映像の身振りや手振りも
参考にして発声してみましょう。

Unit 2

The Mystery of the Declining Bee Population in Japan

ミツバチは人間と深いかかわりのある昆虫です。ハチミツの採取はもちろんのこと、イチゴ、メロン、スイカ等の作物の花粉交配用昆虫としても欠かせない存在です。そんなミツバチが今、日本を含む世界中で減少しています。一体なぜミツバチは減少しているのでしょうか。その謎に迫ってみましょう。

Keywords Check

online audio

Choose the correct definition in Japanese for each word.
それぞれの単語の意味を選択肢から選びましょう。

DL 12　CD 1-12

1. pollination	[ ]	2. horticultural	[ ]
3. questionnaire	[ ]	4. in-depth	[ ]
5. parasitic	[ ]	6. vulnerable	[ ]
7. pathogen	[ ]	8. infectious	[ ]
9. epidemiological	[ ]	10. geographical	[ ]

---

a. 疫学の　**b.** 綿密な　**c.** 病原菌　**d.** 園芸の　**e.** 感染性の
f. 地理的な　**g.** 花粉交配　**h.** アンケート　**i.** 傷つきやすい　**j.** 寄生の

▶️ Watch the Presentation (1st Viewing) online/video

Watch the presentation and answer T(true) or F(false) for each of the following sentences.

プレゼンテーション映像を通しで観て、次の文が正しければ T を、そうでなければ F を選びましょう。

1. The topic of the presentation is the drop in the bee population in Japan. [T / F]

2. The presentation refers to a recent survey of farmers in Japan. [T / F]

3. The presentation talks about research into honeybee pathogen infection.

[T / F]

4. Knowing the reasons for the bee population decline, beekeepers can
   now overcome the problem by themselves. [T / F]

▶️ Focus for Better Understanding (2nd Viewing)

online/video online/audio

Watch three short parts of the presentation for a closer understanding and answer the questions.

次にプレゼンテーション映像をパートごとに観て、それぞれの問題に答えましょう。

Part I DL 13 CD 1-13

What did the questionnaire and interview survey find?

a. The declining bee population was caused by parasitic mites and agricultural chemicals.

b. The declining bee population was caused by many infectious pathogens.

c. The declining bee population was caused by genetic mutation.

d. The declining bee population was caused by the sudden death of queen bees.

Part II DL 14 CD 1-14

In the research, how many viruses were detected in all samples?

a. two viruses

b. five viruses

c. seven viruses

d. four viruses

Considering the results of recent studies, which is most likely to explain the declining bee population?

a. infection

b. agricultural chemicals

c. parasitic mites

d. a combination of the above-mentioned

Useful Phrases

Choose appropriate words from the box to complete each sentence.

日本語に合うように下線部に入る語句を語群から組み合わせて選び、文を完成させましょう（語群では文頭に来る語も小文字で始めています）。

1.「～に加えて」

Today, _____ honey production, bees also play an important role in the pollination of horticultural plants.

2.「～によって引き起こされた」

The survey found that the drop in the bee population _____ parasitic mites as well as the impact of agricultural chemicals used by farmers.

3.「この発表では～を検討してきました」

_____, we _____ recent research into the bee population in Japan.

4.「この問題に対する解決は～です」

_____ beyond the scope of beekeepers alone.

> caused / the solution / in / have examined / addition / was /
> this presentation / in / this problem / is / by / to / to

Summarize the Presentation

DL 16~20   ● CD 1-16 ~ ● CD 1-20

Read the summary of the presentation and fill in the blanks to complete the sentences for each slide.

スライドを参考に、空所に適語を入れプレゼンテーションの要約を完成させましょう。

1.

What's coming?
1. Results of recent research
2. Discussion of causes

Bee populations are steadily (^{1}) throughout the world. But why are the (^{2}) disappearing? In this presentation, we'll first look at (^{3}) (   ) in Japan and then try to determine the (^{4}) of this phenomenon.

2.

Results
Mites   Agricultural chemicals
⬇
~~Bees~~

Let's begin by examining the findings of an interview and questionnaire survey. In the survey, it was (^{5}) that the drop in the (^{6}) (   ) was caused by parasitic mites (^{7}) (   ) (   ) the impact of agricultural chemicals used by farmers.

3.

Results
Infected!
2 viruses in all

Now let us consider research into honeybee pathogen infection. In the research, honeybees were collected from beekeepers throughout Japan, and (^{8}) for seven key viruses known to cause diseases. Two of the seven tested viruses were detected in (^{9}) (   ), while some samples contained as many as five (^{10}).

4.

Discussion

Mites / Agricultural chemicals
+
Viral infection

⬇

Disease

So how can this help us solve the mystery of the declining bee population? It may be that the impact of parasitic mites and (11   ) (   ), as (12   ) in the questionnaire and interview survey, has affected the ability of bees to fight off viruses and avoid (13   ).

5.

Summary

- A chain of factors involved

- Cooperation between farmers & beekeepers required

In this presentation, we have examined recent research into the bee population in Japan and looked at reasons for the population decline. We have seen that the cause is likely to be a (14   ) (   ) (   ). The (15   ) to this problem is beyond the scope of beekeepers alone. It (16   ) a coordinated effort from farmers and beekeepers (17   ) (   ) (   ) find ways to improve the health of bees and restore the bee population to its proper level.

プレゼンテーションの原稿と話ことば

Presentation Tips

　プレゼンテーションは、話しことばで伝えます。だからといって、思い付きをその場で話せばよいというものではありません。とくに外国語で話す場合は、準備として、必ず原稿を作ってください。さもないと、なんと言えばよいか考えるのに手間取ってとても効率の悪いことになり、時間が足りなくなります。しかし、原稿を用意するのは、原稿を読むためではありません。原稿を棒読みで読み上げるプレゼンテーションはとてもわかりづらいです。

　では、何のために原稿を作るのかというと、言いたいことをどう表現すれば良いかを事前に準備するためです。思考を言語化するためです。とくに外国語で行う場合は上手な表現になるように手間を惜しまず何度でも書き直しをしてください。

　自分が話すことをイメージして原稿を書きましょう。聞いていてわかりやすいように、複雑な構文は避け、短く簡潔なセンテンスを書くようにしましょう。一息で言えるくらいの長さだと話しやすいです。そして、できた原稿を、少なくとも3回は音読してください。

　話すスピードは、1分間100語が目安です。音読して、どう言えば良いか慣れたところで、次は、原稿なしでアウトライン程度のメモを使って3回練習してください。実際の発表が原稿と違っていてもかまいません。その場の勢いで話をした方が臨場感があってよいプレゼンテーションになります。

▶️ Dictation and Shadowing

Step 1 Listen and complete the sentences with suitable words. 🎧 DL 21 ⦿ CD 1-21
音声を聞いて、空所に適切な語を入れましょう。

1. _____ _____ _____ _____ the findings of a

recent nationwide survey of beekeepers in Japan.

2. This conclusion _____ _____ _____ _____

_____ _____ suggesting that bees are highly vulnerable to

disease and the effects of pesticides.

3. _____ _____ _____ _____

_____ honeybee pathogen infection.

4. So _____ _____ _____ _____ viral

infection alone could have caused the mass disappearance of bees.

Step 2 Following the video directions, practice A to D.
映像の指示にしたがって、A ～ D の練習をしましょう。

A Say the sentences aloud for Step 1 with audio and text.
Step 1 の文を映像（テキストと音声）と一緒に発声しましょう。

B Say them aloud with the excerpted videos (with subtitles).
Step 1 の文を映像（字幕）と一緒に発声しましょう。

C Say them aloud with the excerpted videos (with only partially completed subtitles).
Step 1 の文を映像（一部以外はすべて空白の字幕）と
一緒に発声しましょう。

D Say them aloud with the excerpted videos (no subtitles).
Step 1 の文を映像（字幕なし）と一緒に発声しましょう。

映像の身振りや手振りも
参考にして発声してみましょう。

Unit 3

Sports in Which Being Small is an Advantage

フィギュアスケートを見ていて、何か気づいたことはありませんか？　ほかの競技に比べて日本人がメダルを取ったり上位に入賞したりすることが多いと思いませんか？　なぜでしょう？　巨大タンカーが舵を切ってもなかなかカーブできないのと同じ原理が働いているのです。

Keywords Check

online audio

Choose the correct definition in Japanese for each word.
それぞれの単語の意味を選択肢から選びましょう。

DL 22　　CD 1-22

1. rotation	[　]	2. angular	[　]
3. determine	[　]	4. inertia	[　]
5. effort	[　]	6. axis	[　]
7. concentrate	[　]	8. Axel	[　]
9. output	[　]	10. opposite	[　]

---

a. 正反対（の）　**b.** 労力　**c.** 決める　**d.** 慣性　**e.** 角度の　**f.** 軸　**g.** 集中する
h. アクセル（ジャンプの一種）　**i.** 出力　**j.** 回転

17

▶️ Watch the Presentation (1st Viewing)

online / video

Watch the presentation and answer T(true) or F(false) for each of the following sentences.

プレゼンテーション映像を通して観て、次の文が正しければ T を、そうでなければ F を選びましょう。

1. The main topic of this presentation is the important reasons why successful figure skaters are small. [T / F]

2. When a figure skater jumps, they immediately pull their legs in tight so that they can jump higher. [T / F]

3. Midori Ito was able to perform the triple Axel for the first time in the world because she was the smallest figure skater ever. [T / F]

4. Physics shows that a heavier and smaller object rotates faster. [T / F]

▶️ Focus for Better Understanding (2nd Viewing)

online / video   online / audio

Watch three short parts of the presentation for a closer understanding and answer the questions.

次にプレゼンテーション映像をパートごとに観て、それぞれの問題に答えましょう。

Part I

🎧 DL 23   💿 CD 1-23

In the presentation, what is a common characteristic of sports in which it is advantageous to be small?

a. They all relate to throwing an object.

b. They all involve running for a long distance.

c. They all concern spinning in the air.

d. They all require spinning on the ground.

figure skater jumps,

ax

Part II

🎧 DL 24   💿 CD 1-24

What do skaters have to do to succeed in performing multiple-rotation jumps?

a. They wear light skate shoes.

b. They jump high to maintain a long air time and spin rapidly.

c. They jump high to lengthen air time and spin clockwise.

d. They spread their hands in the air.

Part III

In whatever sport you try, what is the significant point to succeed?

a. You have to strengthen muscles through training.

b. You need to find more than one coach to direct you.

c. You had better compete against foreign athletes.

d. You have to study physics to learn the mechanism of sustaining power.

Useful Phrases

Choose appropriate words from the box to complete each sentence.

日本語に合うように下線部に入る語句を語群から組み合わせて選び、文を完成させましょう（語群では文頭に来る語も小文字で始めています）。

1.「〜のこととなると」

_____ sports, larger people generally have an advantage.

2.「〜に共通する特徴は」

_____ these sports is that they all involve spinning in the air.

3.「〜をまとめたいと思います」

_____ today's talk.

4.「〜において成功するカギは」

_____ sports is building muscle through strength training and selecting a sport in which you can take advantage of your particular body type.

> to success / the key / to / comes / characteristic of / I would /
> when it / summarize / in / the common / like to

Summarize the Presentation

DL 26~30　　CD 1-26 ~ CD 1-30

Read the summary of the presentation and fill in the blanks to complete the sentences for each slide.

スライドを参考に、空所に適語を入れプレゼンテーションの要約を完成させましょう。

1.

Sports where it is Advantageous to be Small

- Gymnastics
- Figure skating
- Diving

When it comes to sports, larger people generally (¹　　　　) (　　　) (　　　　　　), but there are some sports where it is (²　　　　　) to be small, (³　　　　) (　　　) gymnastics, figure skating and diving. Today, I would like to talk about figure skating and why it is (⁴　　　　　　) for figure skaters to be small.

2.

Figure Skating

The smaller the body, the faster the rotation.

In figure skating, there has been (⁵　　　　　) (　　　　) (　　　　　) (　　　　　) on how many times an athlete can successfully perform a triple jump. Skaters jump high to increase air time and spin quickly. How do you increase the speed (⁶　　　) which you turn? That secret has a key: (⁷　　　　) (　　　) the body, (⁸　　　　) (　　　) the rotation.

3.

When a figure skater jumps,

height
axis

When a figure skater jumps, they immediately (⁹　　　　　　　) their arms in tight to their body. They are reducing the moment of inertia (¹⁰　　　　　) (　　　　　　) they can spin faster. In figure skating, it is advantageous to be physically smaller, (¹¹　　　　　) that is not all it takes to be successful. Muscular strength for jumping is (¹²　　　　　) essential. A person can achieve more air time (¹³　　　　　) jumping higher, (¹⁴　　　　　) more rotations possible.

4.

Two factors in
multiple-rotation jumps

1. Size: smaller ➡ faster
   moment of inertia

2. Power: stronger ➡ higher

Today we (^{15}) at figure skating as an example and considered (^{16}) being small is an advantage in some sports. The key concept was "(^{17}) (   ) (   )." But, you can't win just by being (^{18}). You have to engage in strength training (^{19}) (   ) (   ) increase your power output.

5.

Summary: Key to Success
in Sports

• Large or small: different sports require different sized athletes.
• In either case, power output is important.

⬇

1. Build muscle through strength training.
2. Select a sport in which you can take advantage of your body type.

I would like to (^{20}) today's talk. The (^{21}) (   ) (   ) in sports is building muscle (^{22}) strength training and selecting a sport in which you can (^{23}) (   ) (   ) your particular body type.

スライドの作成（1）　テキスト

Presentation Tips

　スライドの英語表現は短く簡潔にしましょう。1枚のスライドに多くの情報を詰め込み過ぎず、原則1枚のスライドは1つのトピックにしましょう。詳細な説明は口頭で行うわけですからスライドの文字情報は減らすようにします。そのためにはセンテンスではなくキーワードを使ったフレーズにしましょう。文脈から想定できる主語や、冠詞などの機能語などは省略し、情報を伝えるのに必要な語句に絞ります。また要点をまとめて箇条書きにする際には、表現に統一感を持たせるようにしましょう。

●悪いスライド例

Two factors in multiple-rotation jumps

• If two skaters of different sizes were to jump, the smaller one's mass would be more closely concentrated around the axis of rotation and would also weigh less, resulting in a smaller moment of inertia and thus a faster rotation.

• There is another factor in successfully performing a multiple-rotation jump, namely the height of the jump. A person can achieve more air time by jumping higher, making more rotations possible.

●良いスライド例

Two factors in
multiple-rotation jumps

1. Size: smaller ➡ faster
   moment of inertia

2. Power: stronger ➡ higher

▶ Dictation and Shadowing

online / video

Step 1   Listen and complete the sentences with suitable words.   🎧 DL 31   ◎ CD 1-31
音声を聞いて、空所に適切な語を入れましょう。

1. _____ _____ _____ _____ _____ _____

   _____ ____ how many times an athlete can successfully perform a triple jump.

2. The same explanation _____ _____ _____ _____ _____

   _____ figure skating.

3. _____ _____ _____ _____ _____

   successfully performing a multiple-rotation jump, namely the height of the jump.

4. _____ _____ _____ sport you are talking about, the

   power output of your muscles is important.

Step 2   Following the video directions, practice A to D.
映像の指示にしたがって、A ～ D の練習をしましょう。

A Say the sentences aloud for Step 1 with audio and text.
Step 1 の文を映像（テキストと音声）と一緒に発声しましょう。

B Say them aloud with the excerpted videos (with subtitles).
Step 1 の文を映像（字幕）と一緒に発声しましょう。

C Say them aloud with the excerpted videos (with only partially completed subtitles).
Step 1 の文を映像（一部以外はすべて空白の字幕）と
一緒に発声しましょう。

D Say them aloud with the excerpted videos (no subtitles).
Step 1 の文を映像（字幕なし）と一緒に発声しましょう。

顔の表情もバリエーション
豊かに発声してみましょう。

22

Unit 4

Stargazing and Its Enthusiasts

あなたの街から夜空に輝く星が見えますか？　都市部に住んでいても、ちょっと足を延ばせば星の輝きを楽しむことができるかもしれません。時にはスマホの画面から目を離し、夜空の星を見上げてみませんか？

Keywords Check

online audio

DL 32　CD 1-32

Choose the correct definition in Japanese for each word.
それぞれの単語の意味を選択肢から選びましょう。

1. spectacular	[　]	2. artificial	[　]
3. constellation	[　]	4. visible	[　]
5. observe	[　]	6. astronomer	[　]
7. pollution	[　]	8. hemisphere	[　]
9. galaxy	[　]	10. celestial	[　]

> **a.** 天空の　**b.** 壮大な　**c.** 人工の　**d.** 目に見える　**e.** 星座
> **f.** 汚染　**g.** 観測する　**h.** 天文学者　**i.** 地球の半球　**j.** 銀河

▶️ Watch the Presentation (1st Viewing)

Watch the presentation and answer T(true) or F(false) for each of the following sentences.
プレゼンテーション映像を通して観て、次の文が正しければ T を、そうでなければ F を選びましょう。

1. Most of the stars in the Milky Way are bright enough for us to see with the naked eye. [T / F]

2. In order to minimize the effect of light pollution, you need to go as high in elevation as possible. [T / F]

3. Most stargazing enthusiasts go as far as traveling to the Antarctic in search of truly dark night skies. [T / F]

4. Familiar constellations in the northern hemisphere look different when you observe them from the southern hemisphere. [T / F]

▶️ Focus for Better Understanding (2nd Viewing)

Watch three short parts of the presentation for a closer understanding and answer the questions.
次にプレゼンテーション映像をパートごとに観て、それぞれの問題に答えましょう。

Part I
🎧 DL 33 💿 CD 1-33

Why was Comet Holmes witnessed in 2007 only by stargazing enthusiasts and not by ordinary people?

a. Because it can only be seen by the naked eye in rural areas but not in cities.

b. Because its appearance was not reported on news headlines.

c. Because its light was not bright enough to reach the Earth in 2007.

d. Because the moon was in a position that hid the comet.

Part II
🎧 DL 34 💿 CD 1-34

Why is there less light pollution in Australia?

a. Because the air in Australia has much more vapor compared to other countries.

b. Because the night sky in Australia has fewer bright stars.

c. Because the size of big cities in Australia is smaller than those in the northern hemisphere.

d. Because the night sky in Australia has more stars and galaxies than that of the northern hemisphere.

Part III

Which statement is true about the night sky in Australia?

a. You see many celestial objects which are not seen in the northern hemisphere.

b. You see all of the familiar constellations upside down.

c. You see none of the constellations you can observe from Japan.

d. You see Eta Carinae in a different direction compared to the sky in the northern hemisphere.

Useful Phrases

Choose appropriate words from the box to complete each sentence.

日本語に合うように下線部に入る語句を語群から組み合わせて選び、文を完成させましょう（語群では文頭に来る語も小文字で始めています）。

1.「お話しする機会を」

Thank you _____ here today.

2.「～を通してでさえ辛うじて見える程度」

In cities, Comet Holmes was _____, _____
a powerful amateur telescope.

3.「遥かに明るい月は言うまでもなく」

Most of the stars are much fainter than planets like Venus and Jupiter, _____
_____ Moon.

4.「上下逆さまに見える」

Orion, for example, _____!

> let / to be / to speak / down / visible / the much / through / for /
> alone / even / brighter / barely / appears / upside / the chance

Summarize the Presentation

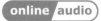

DL 36~40   CD 1-36 ~ CD 1-40

Read the summary of the presentation and fill in the blanks to complete the sentences for each slide.

スライドを参考に、空所に適語を入れプレゼンの要約を完成させましょう。

1.

I would like to talk to you about stargazing. And about stargazing (¹   ) who fly (²   ) (   ) (   ) to Australia to enjoy (³   ) night skies.

2.

In built-up areas where there are so many (⁴   ) sources of light, there are many things we cannot see in the night skies. In the fall of 2007 a bright comet, named Comet Holmes, was discovered in the constellation of Perseus. For months this comet remained visible with the (⁵   ) (   ) from

(⁶   ) locations. But in cities Comet Holmes was barely visible.

3.

In order to (⁷   ) the effect of (⁸   ) (   ) you need firstly to go as far away from big cities as possible and secondly to go as high in (⁹   ) as possible.

4.

Why Australia?

•Less vapor and light pollution

•The southern-hemisphere sky

Image by NASA

Some stargazing enthusiasts go as far as traveling to Australia. There are two reasons for this. The first is the (^10   ) of observing conditions. Australia is mostly a (^11   ), which means the air is (^12   ) and there is much (^13   ) (   ) that contributes to brightening of the night sky. The second reason is what you see in the sky. From the (^14   ) (   ), the Magellanic clouds are easily observable.

5.

Discover the beauty and the grandeur of the Australian sky!

Emu

Image by NASA

Australian Aborigines saw an emu in the (^15   ) (   ). But they weren't so interested in connecting bright stars and (^16   ) (   ) (   ) constellations. You may wonder why. To find out you have to go to Australia and see the starry night sky with your own eyes. I think that you will be (^17   ) (   ) by the beauty and the (^18   ) of it.

スライドの作成（2）スタイル

　スライドはプレゼンテーションの内容を「視覚的」に伝える役割を担う重要な資料です。言葉では伝わりにくい事柄も、一目見てわかる視覚情報を上手く取り入れることで解決できます。手順や関係性を図式化したり、数値をグラフ化したりすることで、情報が伝わり易くなります。図表については細かすぎて何が書いてあるのかわからないのでは困ります。必要な情報を厳選し、ある程度、簡素化して表示するようにしましょう。フォントは見やすいゴシック体を用い、フォントサイズは少し離れたところからでも判読できる程度の大きさにします。強調したいキーワードにはフォントカラーを使い分ければわかり易くなります。ただし、アニメーションなどの特殊効果は、見ている方の気が散って内容に集中できない場合もありますので使い過ぎないようにしましょう。

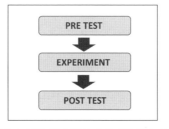

▶️ Dictation and Shadowing

online video

Step 1 Listen and complete the sentences with suitable words.
音声を聞いて、空所に適切な語を入れましょう。　　🎧 DL 41　💿 CD 1-41

1. _____ _____ _____, the large majority of Japanese

   people live in cities.

2. _____ _____ _____ _____ _____

   the quality of observing conditions.

3. Moreover, _____ _____ _____ the metropolitan

   centers are relatively small helps minimize the level of light pollution.

4. Also, familiar constellations _____ _____ from the southern

   hemisphere.

Step 2 Following the video directions, practice A to D.
映像の指示にしたがって、A 〜 D の練習をしましょう。

A Say the sentences aloud for Step 1 with audio and text.
Step 1 の文を映像（テキストと音声）と一緒に発声しましょう。

B Say them aloud with the excerpted videos (with subtitles).
Step 1 の文を映像（字幕）と一緒に発声しましょう。

C Say them aloud with the excerpted videos (with only partially completed subtitles).
Step 1 の文を映像（一部以外はすべて空白の字幕）と
一緒に発声しましょう。

D Say them aloud with the excerpted videos (no subtitles).
Step 1 の文を映像（字幕なし）と一緒に発声しましょう。

映像の身振りや手振りも
参考にして発声してみましょう。

28

Dendrochronology and the *Kiso Hinoki* Cypress

木を切ると現れる年輪をじっくりと観察してみたことはありますか？ 古い樹木の年輪は長い年月をかけて形成され、日本には樹齢 1000 年を越す木もあります。何重にも連なった年輪は、私たちに何を語るのでしょう。

Keywords Check

online audio

Choose the correct definition in Japanese for each word.
それぞれの単語の意味を選択肢から選びましょう。

DL 42　CD 1-42

1. cypress [　]
2. concentration [　]
3. nuclear [　]
4. neutron [　]
5. nitrogen [　]
6. absorb [　]
7. carbon dioxide [　]
8. accelerator [　]
9. discrepancy [　]
10. accurate [　]

a. 窒素　**b.** 吸収する　**c.** 二酸化炭素　**d.** 加速器　**e.** 正確な
f. 核兵器の　**g.** ヒノキ　**h.** 濃度　**i.** 中性子　**j.** 相違

▶️ Watch the Presentation (1st Viewing)

Watch the presentation and answer T(true) or F(false) for each of the following sentences.

プレゼンテーション映像を通しで観て、次の文が正しければ T を、そうでなければ F を選びましょう。

1. The main topic of the presentation is how to measure the age of trees.　　[T / F]

2. As part of the experiment, scientists checked the ratio of H_2O in the air.　　[T / F]

3. Nuclear tests change the proportion of Carbon 14 concentration in the growth rings.　　[T / F]

4. The presentation describes a technique of identifying specific years in the growth rings of different trees.　　[T / F]

▶️ Focus for Better Understanding (2nd Viewing)

Watch three short parts of the presentation for a closer understanding and answer the questions.

次にプレゼンテーション映像をパートごとに観て、それぞれの問題に答えましょう。

Part I

Why do the growth rings of a tree record the concentration of Carbon 14?

a. Because a tree releases Carbon 14 into the air when it is cut.

b. Because nuclear explosions affect trees.

c. Because a tree takes in carbon isotopes from the air as it grows.

d. Because the concentration of Carbon 14 changes the growth rate of a tree.

Part II

How do the scientists measure the concentration of Carbon 14 in growth rings?

a. by nuclear testing

b. by cutting the tree and recycling it

c. by using a particle accelerator

d. by measuring the circulation of Carbon 14

Part III

Which statement is true about the width of growth rings?

a. It can vary due to climate and natural disasters each year.

b. It is fixed so that the pattern of growth rings can be used as a yardstick.

c. It increases at a constant rate as the tree grows.

d. It has a specific rate according to the kind of tree.

Useful Phrases

Choose appropriate words from the box to complete each sentence.

日本語に合うように下線部に入る語句を語群から組み合わせて選び、文を完成させましょう（語群では文頭に来る語も小文字で始めています）。

1.「～を見てみましょう」

_____ the correlation between the concentration of carbon isotope in a tree and the age of the tree.

2.「常に」

Meanwhile, living trees exchange air and carbon _____ _____.

3.「このようにして」

_____, we can determine the age of a tree.

4.「～を説明しました」

In today's presentation, I _____ the way in which changes in the environment affect the concentration of the carbon isotope in trees.

> basis / at / on / described / continuous / a / look /
> this way / in / let's / have

Summarize the Presentation

DL 46~50   CD 1-46 ~ CD 1-50

Read the summary of the presentation and fill in the blanks to complete the sentences for each slide.

スライドを参考に、空所に適語を入れプレゼンテーションの要約を完成させましょう。

1.

Today's topics

- How can the age of trees be determined?
- How can the age of the *Kiso Hinoki* cypress be used?

Today I will be describing a (¹   ) for accurately (²   ) the age of giant forest trees such as the *Kiso Hinoki* (³   ).

2.

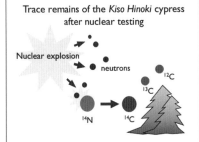

Trace remains of the *Kiso Hinoki* cypress after nuclear testing

Nuclear explosion

neutrons

¹²C

¹³C

¹⁴N   ¹⁴C

First, let's look at the (⁴   ) between the concentration of (⁵   ) isotope in a tree and the age of the tree.

3.

Accurate ¹⁴C dating

- ¹²C : ¹³C : ¹⁴C = unchanged, but with small discrepancies
- Carbon content of trees of known ages
- Nagoya U. has accurate data for the last 800 years

In this way, we can determine the (⁶   ) of a tree by studying changes in Carbon 14 concentrations in the growth rings. The relative (⁷   ) of Carbon 12, Carbon 13 and Carbon 14 in the atmosphere are similar in any given year, but there are small but significant (⁸   ) that must be included in the carbon dating calculations.

4.

Growth ring dendrochronology

"yardstick"
1790 1800 1805 ...   1790 1800 1805 1810

If we overlap the (^{9}) (   ) from a number of trees growing at (^{10}) times, we can identify a general trend in the width of growth rings over an extended period. This trend is known as the "standard curve." The standard curve is like a yardstick for growth rings. It allows us to (^{11}) the

age of a piece of wood by (^{12}) its growth ring pattern to the standard curve.

5.

Conclusions

- Measuring concentration of ^{14}C in trees
- *Kiso Hinoki* cypress as a yardstick of a tree's age

In today's presentation I have described (^{13}) (   ) in which changes in the environment (^{14}) growth and the (^{15}) of the carbon isotope Carbon 14 in trees (^{16}) (   ) the *Kiso Hinoki* cypress.

他人のアイデアや文章を使用する際に気を付けること　*Presentation Tips*

　説得力のあるプレゼンテーションをするために、他者の書いた文章や資料を利用することが多くあります。しかし、引用のルールを無視して他の人のアイデアや文章を勝手に使用してはいけません。以下のケースはどこが不適切でしょうか。

　①他の本で見つけた引用を、元の本を読まないでそのまま引用した

　②引用した箇所に著者名のみのせた

　③引用した箇所のスライドに著者名と出版年をのせた

①は「孫引き」といいます。元の本を確認しましょう。②引用した際には、著者名と出版年も明記しましょう（直接引用の場合はページも明記）。③さらに、最後のスライドに、参考文献（References）のページを加えましょう。

　プレゼンテーションでは、上手く引用しつつ「自分」の考えや意見を「自分」の言葉を使って発表することが重要です。

▶◀ Dictation and Shadowing

online/video

Step 1 Listen and complete the sentences with suitable words.
音声を聞いて、空所に適切な語を入れましょう。 🎧 DL 51 💿 CD 1-51

1. Today I _____ _____ _____ a technique for accurately
   determining the age of giant forest trees such as the *kiso hinoki* cypress.

2. _____ _____ _____, I will explain how changes in
   the carbon isotope concentration correlate with age dating.

3. Finally, _____ _____ _____ how the age of a given
   tree can be used to determine the ages of other trees.

4. _____ _____ _____, the concentration of Carbon 14
   in the atmosphere increases.

Step 2 Following the video directions, practice A to D.
映像の指示にしたがって、A ～ D の練習をしましょう。

A Say the sentences aloud for Step 1 with audio and text.
Step 1 の文を映像（テキストと音声）と一緒に発声しましょう。

B Say them aloud with the excerpted videos (with subtitles).
Step 1 の文を映像（字幕）と一緒に発声しましょう。

C Say them aloud with the excerpted videos (with only
partially completed subtitles).
Step 1 の文を映像（一部以外はすべて空白の字幕）と
一緒に発声しましょう。

D Say them aloud with the excerpted videos (no subtitles).
Step 1 の文を映像（字幕なし）と一緒に発声しましょう。

映像の身振りや手振りも
参考にして発声してみましょう。

Unit 6

The Seasonal Adaptation of Animals

生き物は、毎年正確に春を感知して、食料が豊富で気温の温暖な季節に子供や卵を産みます。その一方で、私たちはスーパーで一年中新鮮な卵を買うことができます。どうして年中卵を買うことができるのでしょう？　このユニットでは、生物の季節を読み取る仕組みとそれを利用した食糧生産について取り上げます。

Keywords Check

online audio

Choose the correct definition in Japanese for each word.
それぞれの単語の意味を選択肢から選びましょう。

DL 52　　CD 1-52

1. reproduction	[　　]	2. pregnancy	[　　]
3. genetically	[　　]	4. vernal equinox	[　　]
5. summer solstice	[　　]	6. organ	[　　]
7. one-hundred-fold	[　　]	8. avian	[　　]
9. unraveling	[　　]	10. trigger	[　　]

> **a.** 遺伝子学的に　**b.** 夏至　**c.** 100 倍　**d.** 解明する　**e.** 鳥類の
> **f.** 器官　**g.** 誘発する　**h.** 生殖　**i.** 妊娠期間　**j.** 春分

▶️ Watch the Presentation (1st Viewing)

(online video)

Watch the presentation and answer T(true) or F(false) for each of the following sentences.

プレゼンテーション映像を通して観て、次の文が正しければ T を、そうでなければ F を選びましょう。

1. The main topic of this presentation is how animals survive through winter. [T / F]

2. Animals need to start mating when food is plentiful. [T / F]

3. Birds show a greater reaction to change in day length than any other creatures.

[T / F]

4. The presentation gives the reason why we can eat egg year-round. [T / F]

▶️ Focus for Better Understanding (2nd Viewing)

(online video)   (online audio)

Watch three short parts of the presentation for a closer understanding and answer the questions.

次にプレゼンテーション映像をパートごとに観て、それぞれの問題に答えましょう。

Part I

Why is it important for animals to sense the season?

a. They need to raise their young at a time when food is becoming scarce.

b. They can find all sorts of foodstuffs throughout the year.

c. They need to put off reproduction until food is plentiful.

d. They need to give birth in a season when food is plentiful.

Part II

Which of the following is NOT reliable for sensing the season?

a. temperature

b. vernal equinox

c. summer solstice

d. day length

Part III

Why do birds adjust the size of their sexual organs in line with the breeding season?

a. The breeding season of birds is shorter than that of any other animal.

b. Birds must usually keep their body weight as light as possible to enable flight.

c. Birds are the most sensitive creatures to seasonal changes.

d. The size of sexual organs is important for breeding.

Useful Phrases

Choose appropriate words from the box to complete each sentence.

日本語に合うように下線部に入る語句を語群から組み合わせて選び、文を完成させましょう（語群では文頭に来る語も小文字で始めています）。

1.「～を確実にするために」

_____ their young survive, animals need to give birth in a season when food is plentiful.

2.「最も信頼できる要因ではない」

Temperature and rainfall are _____.

3.「手短に言えば」

_____, day length is an extremely precise indicator of seasonal change.

4.「～について簡単な説明をする」

In this presentation, I've _____ how the seasons trigger changes in physiological functions of certain creatures.

> the most / a simple / in / given / that / to / not / of / reliable /
> ensure / short / explanation / factors

Summarize the Presentation

DL 56~60   CD 1-56 ~ CD 1-60

Read the summary of the presentation and fill in the blanks to complete the sentences for each slide.

スライドを参考に、空所に適語を入れプレゼンテーションの要約を完成させましょう。

1.

Question

How do animals sense the seasons and adapt to seasonal changes?

I'm here today to give you some research findings (^{1}) how animals sense the seasons and (^{2}) (   ) seasonal changes.

2.

Why is it important to sense the seasons?

6 months

Mate in autumn   Give birth in spring

Goats and sheep, whose (^{3}) last about six months, mate in autumn so as to give birth in spring. Animals are (^{4}) (   ) to anticipate the seasons and mate in time to give birth in spring when food is becoming (^{5}) and temperatures are becoming warmer.

3.

How do animals sense the seasonal changes?

unreliable
• Temperature
• Rainfall

reliable
• Day length
  • Vernal/autumnal equinoxes
  • Winter/summer solstices

Compared with temperature or rainfall, the (^{6}) and autumnal equinoxes and winter and summer solstices are much more (^{7}), coming around every year (^{8}) (   ). In short, day length is an extremely precise (^{9}) of seasonal change, and so it makes sense for creatures to use it as a (^{10}).

4.

Example of photoperiodism

Testes of
Japanese
quails

(Normal size)   (Breading season)

7   8   9   10   11   12

The way in which the physiological functions of creatures change in line with the (^{11}) of day or night is known as photoperiodism. Birds (^{12}) their body weight as much as possible to enable flight, and accordingly (^{13}) the size of their sexual organs in line with the (^{14}) (   ).

5.

Contribution

We can produce eggs
year-round by using
artificial light.

This research contributes to
• the advance of biology
• improving food production

In this presentation, I've given a simple explanation of how the seasons (^{15}) changes in (^{16}) (   ) of certain creatures. We hope that this research will (^{17}) to the advancement of biology and to improving (^{18}) (   ).

オンライン素材の利用上の注意

Presentation Tips

　インターネットの発達で画像やイラストなどの素材を入手しやすくなりました。スライドを作成するのに便利になりましたが、いい加減なサイトも掲載されていることがあります。オンラインに掲載されている画像やイラストを利用する際には、信用できるサイトから適切に活用しましょう。また、オンライン素材を安易にコピーしたり、無断で使用すると著作権を侵害することがあります。サイトから画像やイラストを入手し、正しく使うには以下の点に注意してください。

①使用する前に素材の著作権をチェックし、必要なら著作権者に許可を得た上で、著者名、タイトル、URL 等を明記しましょう。
②著作権使用無料（Royalty free）と記してあっても条件がある場合がありますので、必ず確認しましょう。
③出典が曖昧な画像やイラストは利用しないようにしましょう。

▶️ Dictation and Shadowing

online/video

Step 1 Listen and complete the sentences with suitable words.
音声を聞いて、空所に適切な語を入れましょう。　🎧 DL 61　◎ CD 1-61

1. We still _____ _____ _____ _____ of how

   exactly animals sense the seasons and adapt to seasonal changes.

2. I'm _____ _____ _____ _____ you some

   research findings regarding this longstanding mystery.

3. This means that _____ _____ _____ _____

   put off reproduction until food is plentiful.

4. We hope that this research _____ _____ _____ the

   advance of biology and to improving food production.

Step 2 Following the video directions, practice A to D.
映像の指示にしたがって、A〜D の練習をしましょう。

A Say the sentences aloud for Step 1 with audio and text.
Step 1 の文を映像（テキストと音声）と一緒に発声しましょう。

B Say them aloud with the excerpted videos (with subtitles).
Step 1 の文を映像（字幕）と一緒に発声しましょう。

C Say them aloud with the excerpted videos (with only partially completed subtitles).
Step 1 の文を映像（一部以外はすべて空白の字幕）と
一緒に発声しましょう。

D Say them aloud with the excerpted videos (no subtitles).
Step 1 の文を映像（字幕なし）と一緒に発声しましょう。

映像の身振りや手振りも
参考にして発声してみましょう。

Unit 7

Percival Lowell: Pluto, Martians, and the Japanese

太陽系における星の中で、火星は Mars、木星は Jupiter、金星は Venus、では冥王星は英語で何と言うでしょう。冥王星の発見に貢献し、その名前の由来となった人物の活躍を見てみましょう。

Keywords Check

online audio

🎧 DL 62　◎ CD 1-62

Choose the correct definition in Japanese for each word.
それぞれの単語の意味を選択肢から選びましょう。

1. renowned	[　]	2. successor	[　]
3. space probe	[　]	4. speculation	[　]
5. interim	[　]	6. invasion	[　]
7. anthropology	[　]	8. outrageous	[　]
9. dominant	[　]	10. evolution	[　]

> **a.** 侵略　**b.** 良識に反する　**c.** 進化　**d.** 憶測　**e.** 合間
> **f.** 宇宙探査機　**g.** 有名な　**h.** 後継者　**i.** 人類学　**j.** 支配的な

▶◀ Watch the Presentation (1st Viewing)

online / video

Watch the presentation and answer T(true) or F(false) for each of the following sentences.
プレゼンテーション映像を通しで観て、次の文が正しければ T を、そうでなければ F を選びましょう。

1. The main topic of this presentation is the achievements of Percival Lowell. [T / F]

2. Pluto is currently regarded as a planet. [T / F]

3. Lowell's first interest was the solar system. [T / F]

4. Lowell visited Japan in the Meiji era. [T / F]

▶◀ Focus for Better Understanding (2nd Viewing)

online / video   online / audio

Watch three short parts of the presentation for a closer understanding and answer the questions.
次にプレゼンテーション映像をパートごとに観て、それぞれの問題に答えましょう。

Part I

DL 63   CD 1-63

Although Pluto is no longer a planet, the search for Pluto played a significant role in astronomy. Why is this?

a. It's because Clyde Tombaugh finally found Pluto in 1930.

b. It's because the search led to the thorough observation of the solar system.

c. It's because Clyde Tombaugh named the planet in honor of Percival Lowell.

d. It's because Percival Lowell built the Lowell Observatory.

Part II

DL 64   CD 1-64

According to the presentation, what made Lowell build an observatory of his own?

a. Lowell was influenced by Giovanni Schiaparelli's theory of Martian canals.

b. Arizona was an ideal place for astronomical observation.

c. Lowell first wanted to write science fiction books about Mars.

d. NASA couldn't launch space probes until the 1960s.

42

Part III

Judging from the statements in Lowell's book *The Soul of the Far East*, he seemed to look down on the Japanese. Did he really despise the Japanese?

a. No. "Social Darwinism" was not Lowell's idea, but Darwin's.

b. Yes. He regarded the Japanese as far behind in terms of evolution as human beings and he disliked Japan.

c. No, not really. At the time, "Social Darwinism" was just dominant among Western elites.

d. Yes. Many of his statements are outrageous and infuriating because he had such an ideology.

Useful Phrases

Choose appropriate words from the box to complete each sentence.

日本語に合うように下線部に入る語句を語群から組み合わせて選び、文を完成させましょう（語群では文頭に来る語も小文字で始めています）。

1.「広く受け入れられていた」

These books smack of science fiction today, but in his day his views _____
_____.

2.「〜に照らせば」

A large portion of Lowell's writings is outdated _____ the latest scholarship in cultural anthropology.

3.「それに比べ」

_____, *Noto* is a refreshing read even today.

4.「例えば〜を取り上げてみましょう」

_____ the passage from *The Soul of the Far East*.

were / for / contrast / light / instance / accepted / in /
widely / of / in / take

Summarize the Presentation

DL 66~70　CD 1-66 ～ CD 1-70

Read the summary of the presentation and fill in the blanks to complete the sentences for each slide.

スライドを参考に、空所に適語を入れプレゼンテーションの要約を完成させましょう。

1.

Percival Lowell
(1855 – 1916)

1. Launched a project to find Pluto

2. Observed Mars

3. Wrote books on Japan in the Meiji Era

Today, I would like to talk about the person who (^{1}) a project to find Pluto. His name was Percival Lowell. In this presentation, I'll look (^{2}) (   ) at Lowell's main (^{3}).

2.

Project to Find Pluto

After Percival Lowell's death, Clyde Tombaugh took over the search at the Lowell Observatory, and found Pluto in 1930.

P. L. u t o

First, Percival Lowell is credited with launching a search for a new planet outside the (^{4}) of Neptune. Although he did not live long enough to discover Pluto, his (^{5}) at Lowell Observatory, Clyde Tombaugh, kept looking and finally found it in 1930. Tombaugh honored Percival Lowell's efforts by (^{6}) the planet partly based on his initials "P. L." Lowell's interest in Pluto played a significant role in (^{7}).

3.

Observation of Mars

- Lowell Observatory in Arizona
- Books on Mars
  - *Mars: is there life on Mars?* (1895)
  - *Mars and its Canals* (1906)
  - *Mars as the Abode of Life* (1908)

Lowell built an (^{8}) of his own in Arizona and spent many months every year observing Mars. He published maps of Mars' (^{9}), and wrote many books on Mars.

4.

Lowell's Stay in Japan in the 1880s

Wrote three books about Japan:
- *The Soul of the Far East* (1888)
- *Noto: An Unexplored Corner of Japan* (1891)
- *Occult Japan* (1894)

Before he ([10]   ) (   ) astronomy, Percival Lowell made several ([11]   ) (   ) in Japan in the 1880s and wrote three books on Japan.

5.

The Legacy of Percival Lowell

1. Pluto is no longer considered a planet.
2. Martians and their canals do not exist.
3. His views about the Japanese are outdated.

But

1. His works on Japan serve as a good historical document.
2. His works on Mars and Martians inspired his contemporaries.
3. Astronomy was inspired by the existence of Pluto.

So what is the legacy of Percival Lowell? In my opinion, everything. His works on Japan serve as a good ([12]   ) (   ) about Japan in the Meiji era. His works on Mars and Martians inspired his contemporaries to astronomy. And, astronomy itself was inspired by the existence of Pluto, which led to the more extensive understanding of our ([13]   ) (   ) which we have today. Percival Lowell was one of the greatest examples of human ([14]   ) (   ).

図表・グラフ

Presentation Tips

　プレゼンテーションを大いに助ける大切な道具が図表・グラフと言った視覚的な情報です。特に母語ではない英語によるプレゼンテーションにおいては、その重要性はさらに高まります。いかに少ない説明で図（figure）・表（table）・グラフ（graph, chart）を理解してもらえるかが最も大切です。ここでは特に英語でのプレゼンテーションに特化した図表・グラフの注意点をまとめてみましょう。

① **タイトル（title）で図表・グラフに何が示されているかを簡潔に示しましょう**
② **軸タイトル（axis label）、単位（unit）、凡例（legend）は必ず付けましょう**
③ **図表の説明（caption）もわかりやすく付けましょう**

　図表は多くの情報を提示出来る反面、そこに何が示されているかが明確でないと全く理解されません。あなたの説明を聞き落した聴衆、後からスライドを見直す人にも図表・グラフを理解してもらえるかが重要なポイントです。良い図表は言葉での説明を必要とせず、あなたの英語が不十分でも補ってくれます。

▶ Dictation and Shadowing

online / video

Step 1 Listen and complete the sentences with suitable words. 🎧 DL 71 ◉ CD 1-71
音声を聞いて、空所に適切な語を入れましょう。

1. Today, I would like to talk about the person who _____ _____

_____ to find Pluto.

2. In this presentation, I'll _____ _____ _____ _____

Lowell's main achievements.

3. Today, Pluto _____ _____ _____ _____ _____

a planet.

4. Darwin's theory of evolution continues to be _____ _____

_____ _____ in biology.

Step 2 Following the video directions, practice A to D.
映像の指示にしたがって、A ～ D の練習をしましょう。

A Say the sentences aloud for Step 1 with audio and text.
Step 1 の文を映像（テキストと音声）と一緒に発声しましょう。

B Say them aloud with the excerpted videos (with subtitles).
Step 1 の文を映像（字幕）と一緒に発声しましょう。

C Say them aloud with the excerpted videos (with only partially completed subtitles).
Step 1 の文を映像（一部以外はすべて空白の字幕）と
一緒に発声しましょう。

D Say them aloud with the excerpted videos (no subtitles).
Step 1 の文を映像（字幕なし）と一緒に発声しましょう。

顔の表情もバリエーション
豊かに発声してみましょう。

46

Unit 8

Informal Science Education

皆さんが小・中学校や高校で受けた理科や科学の授業はどのようなものでしたか？　最近、若者たちの科学離れの問題が懸念されています。しかし科学を学ぶのは何も正規の授業の中だけとは限りません。このユニットでは、科学を学ぶ１つのプロジェクトを紹介します。

Keywords Check

online / audio

DL 72　　CD 2-02

Choose the correct definition in Japanese for each word.
それぞれの単語の意味を選択肢から選びましょう。

1. safeguard　　　　[　　]　　　2. worsen　　　　　[　　]

3. hands-on　　　　[　　]　　　4. inquiry　　　　　[　　]

5. interdisciplinary　[　　]　　　6. traditional　　　 [　　]

7. address　　　　　[　　]　　　8. initiative　　　　[　　]

9. scheme　　　　　[　　]　　　10. replacement　　 [　　]

---

a. 取り組む　**b.** 学際的な　**c.** 実際に触れることができる　**d.** 悪くなる
e. 差し替え　**f.** 守る　**g.** 質問　**h.** 従来の　**i.** 計画　**j.** 新構想

▶️ Watch the Presentation (1st Viewing) online / video

Watch the presentation and answer T(true) or F(false) for each of the following sentences.
プレゼンテーション映像を通しで観て、次の文が正しければTを、そうでなければFを選びましょう。

1. In many countries, young people are losing interest in learning science. [T / F]

2. According to an EU report, not only students but also teachers tend to stay away from formal learning. [T / F]

3. The aim of PENCIL is to search for the best possible teaching technique of science education. [T / F]

4. The presenter argues for the replacement of schools by science centers. [T / F]

▶️ Focus for Better Understanding (2nd Viewing)

online / video online / audio

Watch three short parts of the presentation for a closer understanding and answer the questions.
次にプレゼンテーション映像をパートごとに観て、それぞれの問題に答えましょう。

Part I 🎧 DL 73 💿 CD 2-03

According to the presentation, what do most young people like to do?

a. They like to talk with teachers.

b. They like to learn science in school.

c. They like to watch TV and use computers.

d. They like to learn the mechanism of screens.

Part II 🎧 DL 74 💿 CD 2-04

Which of the following is NOT mentioned among the examples of informal learning?

a. excursions

b. hands-on approaches

c. inquiry method learning

d. interdisciplinary presentations

Part III

Which activity is NOT a part of PENCIL?

a. research on informal learning

b. the application of formal learning

c. the cooperation of European countries

b. the improvement of teaching techniques

Useful Phrases

Choose appropriate words from the box to complete each sentence.

日本語に合うように下線部に入る語句を語群から組み合わせて選び、文を完成させましょう（語群では文頭に来る語も小文字で始めています）。

1.「～に関する発表をする」

I'm here to _____ informal science education.

2.「言い換えれば」

_____, in many countries, young people are losing interest in science learning.

3.「前の世代と比較して」

_____, young people nowadays spend increasing amounts of time in front of screens.

4.「締めくくりに」

So, _____, let me summarize the main points of my talk.

> way / a speech / up / generations / previous / it / another / on /
> compared / with / to put / to wrap / present

Summarize the Presentation

DL 76~80   CD 2-06 ~ CD 2-10

Read the summary of the presentation and fill in the blanks to complete the sentences for each slide.

スライドを参考に、空所に適語を入れプレゼンテーションの要約を完成させましょう。

1.

| Today's lecture: |
| **Informal Science Education** |

I'm here to present a speech on informal science education. It's reported that young people are becoming (¹   ) (   ) (   ) interested in learning about the natural sciences. What has caused this (²   ) (   ) (   )?

2.

| **Students' Belief** |
| "Science is difficult" |
| ⬇ |
| **Teachers must change this belief** |

One of the reasons is their belief that "Science is difficult." However, (³   ) (   ) (   ), there is no room for any society to miss the train of scientific innovation. Thus, our (⁴   ) (   ) is to turn around students' belief that "Science is difficult," in order to (⁵   ) the next generation of science teachers and researchers.

3.

| **Toward a resolution: Students** |
| Informal Learning: *hands-on approaches *inquiry method |
| Students' Interest |
| Up |

Young people are becoming more interested in science in informal learning settings. Many science centers and (⁶   )-(   ) museums provide (⁷   )-(   ) approaches, inquiry method learning, and (⁸   ) presentations.

4.

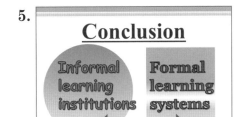

My initiative
PENCIL
the Permanent EuropeaN
Resource Center for
Informal Learning

To (⁹　　　　　) the current situation, I have set up the Permanent European Resource Center for Informal Learning, or "PENCIL" (¹⁰　　　　) (　　　　　　). The aim of project PENCIL is to search for the (¹¹　　　　) (　　　　　) of successful teaching techniques.

5.

Conclusion

Informal learning institutions　　Formal learning systems

Cooperation

Although I have focused on science centers outside formal learning, I don't mean to argue for (¹²　　　　　　) of schools by science centers. Instead, I propose that formal learning systems (¹³　　　　) (　　　　) informal learning institutions outside schools to resolve the (¹⁴　　　　　) (　　　　　　).

数字・数式の読み方

Presentation Tips

　プレゼンテーションでは書き物と違い、数字や数式を声に出して発音することが必要になります。特に理系の学生には必須のことですが、実はあまり習ってはいません。プレゼンテーションの前にどう発音するかをしっかりと予習しておきましょう。例えば、6.02×10^{23} はどう言えば良いでしょうか？（six point oh two times ten to the twenty-third [power]）。簡単な分数 2/5 は two fifths といった言い方は習っているかもしれませんが、a/b を a over b と言うこともあります。英語で書かれた教科書にも数式は出てきますが、数は見ただけでわかってしまい、普段はあえて英語で読み上げたりしていないのではないでしょうか？

　また、日本語で 10 万 5 千が英語では 105 thousand と、桁の取り方が異なるのが難しい点です。英語でプレゼンテーションをしているのになぜか数字だけが日本語になってしまうといった失敗は、特に質問された際の受け答えなど、練習出来ていない場合に多く見られます。普段から数式や数字をどう発音するか、英語で声に出して言ってみるといった練習が大切です。

▶️ Dictation and Shadowing

online / video

Step 1 Listen and complete the sentences with suitable words. 🎧 DL 81 💿 CD 2-11
音声を聞いて、空所に適切な語を入れましょう。

1. Thus our _____ _____ _____ _____ turn around

   students' belief that "Science is difficult."

2. The presentation _____ _____ _____ three parts.

3. So, first, _____ _____ _____ _____ the

   current formal learning situation.

4. I'm _____ that's _____ _____ _____ we

   have now.

Step 2 Following the video directions, practice A to D.
映像の指示にしたがって、A ～ D の練習をしましょう。

A Say the sentences aloud for Step 1 with audio and text.
Step 1 の文を映像（テキストと音声）と一緒に発声しましょう。

B Say them aloud with the excerpted videos (with subtitles).
Step 1 の文を映像（字幕）と一緒に発声しましょう。

C Say them aloud with the excerpted videos (with only partially completed subtitles).
Step 1 の文を映像（一部以外はすべて空白の字幕）と一緒に発声しましょう。

D Say them aloud with the excerpted videos (no subtitles).
Step 1 の文を映像（字幕なし）と一緒に発声しましょう。

映像の身振りや手振りも
参考にして発声してみましょう。

Unit 9

Sympathy and Empathy Among Groups: US Government and Native Americans

同情と共感の違いって何でしょう。実は、この違いを知っていることが、グローバルな人材には欠かせません。このプレゼンテーションを通して、アメリカにおける「同情と共感」の歴史を振り返り、多様な個人・集団が共生していくための鍵を探ってみましょう。

Keywords Check

online audio

Choose the correct definition in Japanese for each word.
それぞれの単語の意味を選択肢から選びましょう。

DL 82　CD 2-12

1. government 　　[　　]　　　2. colonial 　　[　　]

3. settler 　　　　[　　]　　　4. communal 　　[　　]

5. redistribute 　[　　]　　　6. instill 　　　[　　]

7. integration 　　[　　]　　　8. presuppose 　[　　]

9. symbiotic 　　 [　　]　　 10. coexist 　　　[　　]

---

a. 共有の　　**b.** 共存する　　**c.** 融合　　**d.** 政府　　**e.** 再分配する

f. 植民地の　　**g.** 入植者　　**h.** 共生の　　**i.** 前提にする　　**j.** 徐々に教え込む

▶️ Watch the Presentation (1st Viewing)

online / video

Watch the presentation and answer T(true) or F(false) for each of the following sentences.
プレゼンテーション映像を通しで観て、次の文が正しければ T を、そうでなければ F を選びましょう。

1. The Indian Policy of the United States in the second half of the 19th century was characterized by an empathetic approach. [T / F]

2. The Native Americans in the second half of the 19th century were not allowed to use their native languages. [T / F]

3. At the turn of the 20th century, the Indian Policy of the United States took a sympathetic approach. [T / F]

4. For the coexistence of diverse groups, an empathetic approach is more suitable than a sympathetic one. [T / F]

▶️ Focus for Better Understanding (2nd Viewing)

online / video   online / audio

Watch three short parts of the presentation for a closer understanding and answer the questions.
次にプレゼンテーション映像をパートごとに観て、それぞれの問題に答えましょう。

Part I
🎧 DL 83   💿 CD 2-13

Which statement is true of the status of the Native Americans today?

a. They belong to the poorest group in the United States.

b. Their population in the United States is more than 1% of the total population.

c. More than three quarters of them are enjoying a decent standard of living.

d. They are still the target of sympathy.

Part II
🎧 DL 84   💿 CD 2-14

How did the United States try to assimilate the Native Americans in the second half of the 19th century?

a. by splitting communal tribes

b. through an empathetic approach

c. by giving land to them

d. through education and Christianity

Part III

What enabled the Native Americans to govern themselves on reservations in the 1930s?

a. a revival of the Native American languages and religions

b. the formal integration of the Native Americans into the United States in 1924

c. a change in policy of the United States toward the Native Americans

d. the frequent ethnic movements to establish their own government

Useful Phrases

Choose appropriate words from the box to complete each sentence.

日本語に合うように下線部に入る語句を語群から組み合わせて選び、文を完成させましょう（語群では文頭に来る語も小文字で始めています）。

1.「〜を考慮する」

However, this one-sided policy did not _____ the identity of the Native Americans.

2.「貧困に陥った」

As a result, they _____ and by the early 20th century, their population had been decreased significantly.

3.「現在では」

_____, stereotypes of the Indian have been improved, and their identity is more respected.

4.「歴史を振り返る」

When we _____ like this, we can see how the sympathy-based assimilation policy had limits.

> at / at / poverty / back / account / present / into / take / fell /
> look / into / history

Summarize the Presentation

DL 86~90   CD 2-16 ~ CD 2-20

Read the summary of the presentation and fill in the blanks to complete the sentences for each slide.

スライドを参考に、空所に適語を入れプレゼンテーションの要約を完成させましょう。

1.

Sympathy and Empathy
Among Groups:

US Government
and
Native Americans

In this presentation, I shall try to show some of the (^{1}) between (^{2}) (   ) (   ) within group relationships, using the historical relationship between the (^{3}) (   ) and the United States Government as my example.

2.

Native Americans today

Poor minority

✓ 1% of the US population
✓ 1/4 are "poor"

Now let us briefly look at some (^{4}) about today's Native Americans. Their population in the United States is less than 1% of the total (^{5}). And, with more than a (^{6}) of them living below the (^{7}) level, they form the poorest minority group in the States.

3.

19th to early 20th century

Indian policy in US
||
Sympathetic approach

With that, let us (^{8}) (   ) in history. To start with, let us look at the (^{9}) Policy of the United States from the second half of the 19th century to the early 20th. Policy at that time was characterized by a (^{10}) approach. Americans at the time were sympathetic to the circumstances the

Native Americans were in, but they also attempted to change the Native Americans through instilling their own values and lifestyles, (^{11}) (   ) they were the Indians' guardians.

4.

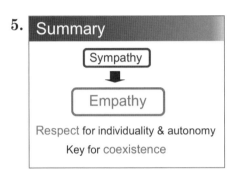

20th century

Assimilation
↓
Empathetic approach

Next, I would like to take a look at the (^{12}) (   ) policy that took place in the 20th century. At the turn of the century, the (^{13}) policy was forced to improve. In other words, it took an (^{14}) approach that took (^{15}) (   ) the needs and voices of the Native Americans.

5.

Summary

Sympathy
↓
Empathy

Respect for individuality & autonomy
Key for coexistence

Empathy is a (^{16}) principle that attempts to (^{17}) individuality and autonomy. Thus, it is the key that allows many diverse groups to (^{18}) without denying each other, even if they are not able to see eye to eye.

シャドーイングでプレゼンテーションの基礎練習   *Presentation Tips*

　プレゼンテーションの基礎練習として、本教科書の動画を使ってシャドーイング練習をしてみましょう。シャドーイングとは、聞こえてきた英語を即座に口に出していく練習法です。ポイントとしては、自分が発表者になったつもりで、できるだけ発音やイントネーションもまねるようにしましょう。はじめは音をまねることに注意しますが、数回練習してからは、意味も思い浮かべながらシャドーイングするようにしましょう。スクリプトは最初は見てもよいですが、その後はできるだけ見ないようにしましょう。何回も口に出すうちに、プレゼンテーションで使う表現が発音やイントネーションも含めて頭に入ってきます。

【シャドーイングに Try!】
このユニットの動画のイントロダクション部分（~ 00:42）を使ってシャドーイング練習をやってみよう（スクリプトは教員が準備します）。
　①**スクリプトを見てシャドーイング（1～2回）**
　②**スクリプトを見ないでシャドーイング（2～3回）**
　③**隣の人にどれだけ言えたかチェックしてもらいましょう**
　　（隣の人はスクリプトを見ながら、言えなかった単語をチェックする）

▶ Dictation and Shadowing

online video

Step 1 Listen and complete the sentences with suitable words. 🎧 DL 91 ⦿ CD 2-21
音声を聞いて、空所に適切な語を入れましょう。

1. _____ _____, let us go back in history and take a look at the

   relationship between the Native Americans and the US Government.

2. _____ _____ _____, let us look at the Indian Policy

   of the United States from the second half of the 19th century to the early 20th.

3. The Native Americans lost their tribal bonds _____ _____

   the land that was their source of spiritual nourishment.

4. Sympathy presupposes that people or groups _____ _____

   _____ _____ _____ one another.

Step 2 Following the video directions, practice A to D.
映像の指示にしたがって、A 〜 D の練習をしましょう。

A Say the sentences aloud for Step 1 with audio and text.
Step 1 の文を映像（テキストと音声）と一緒に発声しましょう。

B Say them aloud with the excerpted videos (with subtitles).
Step 1 の文を映像（字幕）と一緒に発声しましょう。

C Say them aloud with the excerpted videos (with only
partially completed subtitles).
Step 1 の文を映像（一部以外はすべて空白の字幕）と
一緒に発声しましょう。

D Say them aloud with the excerpted videos (no subtitles).
Step 1 の文を映像（字幕なし）と一緒に発声しましょう。

映像の身振りや手振りも
参考にして発声してみましょう。

Unit 10

Is Fear of Snakes Innate?

皆さん、ヘビって怖いですか？　それはなぜですか？　きっと、そんなことを考えたこと
ないですよね。でも理由があるのです。どんな方法で調べるのかにも注目しつつ、人間が
ヘビが怖いと思う理由を探ってみましょう。

Keywords Check

online audio

DL 92　CD 2-22

Choose the correct definition in Japanese for each word.
それぞれの単語の意味を選択肢から選びましょう。

1. lab-reared　　　　[　　] 　　2. nurture　　　　　[　　]

3. reaction　　　　　[　　] 　　4. indicator　　　　[　　]

5. detect　　　　　　[　　] 　　6. odd　　　　　　　[　　]

7. sensitivity　　　　[　　] 　　8. innate　　　　　　[　　]

9. ancestor　　　　　[　　] 　　10. pathway　　　　[　　]

> **a.** 祖先　**b.** 経路　**c.** 指標　**d.** 反応　**e.** 育成　**f.** 生まれつきの
> **g.** 研究所で育った　**h.** 他と違う　**i.** 敏感さ　**j.** 探し当てる

▶ Watch the Presentation (1st Viewing)

Watch the presentation and answer T(true) or F(false) for each of the following sentences.

プレゼンテーション映像を通しで観て、次の文が正しければ T を、そうでなければ F を選びましょう。

1. The presentation talks about why we are scared of snakes.　　[T / F]

2. The presentation looks at some observation research into monkeys born and
reared in the lab.　　[T / F]

3. The presentation looks at recent research that used reaction time to snakes
as an indicator.　　[T / F]

4. It is assumed that our fear of snakes is not innate.　　[T / F]

▶ Focus for Better Understanding (2nd Viewing)

Watch three short parts of the presentation for a closer understanding and answer the questions.

次にプレゼンテーション映像をパートごとに観て、それぞれの問題に答えましょう。

Part I　　🎧 DL 93　💿 CD 2-23

After watching another monkey showing fear of snakes, what changes did the lab-reared monkeys experience?

a. They became aggressive.

b. They started to show fear as well.

c. They did not show any sign of change.

d. They started to nurture another monkey's baby.

Part II　　🎧 DL 94　💿 CD 2-24

What was the result of the experiment on reaction time?

a. Monkeys made more errors detecting snakes than they did detecting flowers.

b. The monkeys detected flowers faster than they detected snakes.

c. There was no difference in the reaction times for the two types of pictures used in
the experiment.

d. The monkeys were quicker at detecting snakes than flowers.

Part III

As part of the evolutionary process, what happened to our ancestors?

a. They developed the ability to see distances.

b. They developed the ability to quickly pick out snakes.

c. They gained the ability to spot beautiful flowers.

d. They learned to help protect each other from snakes.

Useful Phrases

Choose appropriate words from the box to complete each sentence.

日本語に合うように下線部に入る語句を語群から組み合わせて選び、文を完成させましょう（語群では文頭に来る語も小文字で始めています）。

1.「ご覧のように」

_____ here, the monkeys were shown a number of photos of flowers and snakes on a computer screen.

2.「〜から何が言えるでしょうか」

_____ the results of these experiments on reaction time?

3.「これは〜ということを示唆しています」

_____ they were born with this trait.

4.「同じ結論を導き出す」

We can't immediately _____ about innate fear of snakes for humans as we can for monkeys.

---

what / the / suggests / you can / same / see / draw / we say /
can / from / this / conclusion / that / as

Summarize the Presentation

DL 96~100 CD 2-26 ~ CD 2-30

Read the summary of the presentation and fill in the blanks to complete the sentences for each slide.

スライドを参考に、空所に適語を入れプレゼンテーションの要約を完成させましょう。

1.

Is Fear of Snakes Innate?

Good afternoon. Let me begin my presentation by asking you a quick question. Are you (¹   ) (   ) snakes? You are, aren't you? But why? We'll take a look together at some (²   ) (   ) and think about this question.

2.

Observation

Lab-reared monkeys

No fear

First, let's look at some research involving the (³   ) of monkeys born and reared in the (⁴   ). In order to figure out whether the fear observed is something (⁵   ) or something learned, researchers used lab-reared monkeys that had never seen a snake and found that those monkeys showed no obvious signs of (⁶   ) of snakes.

3.

Reaction time as an indicator of fear

Frightening things ➡ **Fast detection**

But do lab-reared monkeys really feel nothing when they see a snake? Actually, recent research has continued investigating fear, using (⁷   ) (   ) to snakes as an (⁸   ). The research showed that the monkeys detected the snakes (⁹   ) than they did the flowers. The researchers also (¹⁰   ) (   ) the same experiment on humans and got the same results.

4.

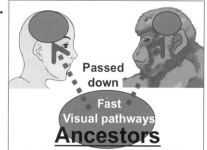

Passed down

Fast Visual pathways

Ancestors

So, what can we say from the research on reaction time? Humans and monkeys share a (^11   ) ancestor, and it is assumed that, as part of the evolutionary process, our (^12   ) developed pathways in the brain for processing visually-received information, to help them survive. These pathways included the (^13   ) to quickly pick out snakes. And this ability has been (^14   ) (   ) to both humans and monkeys as a shared instinct.

5.

Conclusion

Fear of snakes:

- Something innate
- Evolutionary process

Well, now it is time to move on to today's conclusion, which is that not only (^15   ) but also (^16   ) are (^17   ) hard-wired to be afraid of snakes.

ジェスチャーとアイコンタクト

　プレゼンテーションでは、聴衆は発表者の話す内容を聞くだけでなく動きやしぐさも見ています。つまり、ことばだけでなく、ジェスチャーやアイコンタクトも使って内容を伝えることが大切です。例えば、このユニットの動画では、0:22 あたりで「but why」と言いながら大きく手を広げるジェスチャーをしています（写真①）。思わず視線が行きますし、問題提起していることが実によく伝わってきます。また、0:55 あたりで「that had never seen」という際に手ぶりを加えていますが（写真②）、否定のニュアンスがよく伝わります。

　ジェスチャーは数多くありますが、まずはこのユニットで出てくる問題提起や否定のジェスチャーを参考にしてみてください。また、アイコンタクトについては、聴衆の中で左側、中央、右側の３人くらいをあらかじめ決めておいて、プレゼンテーション中にその３人に順番に視線を向けるようにすると会場全体とコンタクトしていることが伝わってよいでしょう。是非、実践してみてください。

①

② vation
o-reared
onkeys

▶️ Dictation and Shadowing

online/video

Step 1 Listen and complete the sentences with suitable words. 🎧 DL 101 💿 CD 2-31
音声を聞いて、空所に適切な語を入れましょう。

1. Let me _____ _____ _____ _____ asking you a

   quick question.

2. In order to _____ _____ whether the fear observed is

   something instinctive or something learned, researchers used lab-reared monkeys

   that had never seen a snake.

3. _____ _____ _____ _____ humans are quicker

   at detecting things that are frightening than things that are not.

4. Now it's time to _____ _____ _____ _____ _____.

Step 2 Following the video directions, practice A to D.
映像の指示にしたがって、A 〜 D の練習をしましょう。

A Say the sentences aloud for Step 1 with audio and text.
Step 1 の文を映像（テキストと音声）と一緒に発声しましょう。

B Say them aloud with the excerpted videos (with subtitles).
Step 1 の文を映像（字幕）と一緒に発声しましょう。

C Say them aloud with the excerpted videos (with only partially completed subtitles).
Step 1 の文を映像（一部以外はすべて空白の字幕）と一緒に発声しましょう。

D Say them aloud with the excerpted videos (no subtitles).
Step 1 の文を映像（字幕なし）と一緒に発声しましょう。

映像の身振りや手振りも
参考にして発声してみましょう。

Emotion of University Students in Daily Life

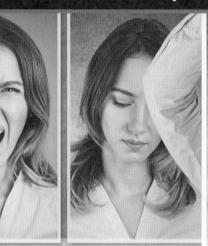

最近嬉しかったことや悲しかったことは何ですか。あまり意識しないかもしれませんが、私たちは日々様々な感情の中で生活しています。このユニットでは、大学生の日常的な感情をその原因とともに研究した結果を紹介しています。

Keywords Check

online audio

Choose the correct definition in Japanese for each word.
それぞれの単語の意味を選択肢から選びましょう。

DL 102　CD 2-32

1. comparison	[ ]	2. gender	[ ]
3. peak	[ ]	4. drowsy	[ ]
5. anticipation	[ ]	6. unemployment	[ ]
7. achievement	[ ]	8. affinity	[ ]
9. trend	[ ]	10. statistical	[ ]

---

a. 親和　**b.** 眠い　**c.** 頂点・最大　**d.** 達成　**e.** 比較
f. 性別　**g.** 予測　**h.** 統計的な　**i.** 失業　**j.** 傾向

▶◀ Watch the Presentation (1st Viewing)

Watch the presentation and answer T(true) or F(false) for each of the following sentences.

プレゼンテーション映像を通しで観て、次の文が正しければ T を、そうでなければ F を選びましょう。

1. The topic of the presentation is the lifestyle of university students. [T / F]

2. The presentation mentions the number of students who participated in the study. [T / F]

3. The study compared the emotions of university students and those of junior high school students. [T / F]

4. In the gender comparison, there were clear-cut differences between males and females. [T / F]

▶◀ Focus for Better Understanding (2nd Viewing)

Watch three short parts of the presentation for a closer understanding and answer the questions.

次にプレゼンテーション映像をパートごとに観て、それぞれの問題に答えましょう。

Part I
🎧 DL 103 ◎ CD 2-33

When are university students more likely to feel angry?

a. when they wake up

b. after the end of lectures

c. during lunch

d. during morning lectures

Part II
🎧 DL 104 ◎ CD 2-34

Which statement is true of causes of emotions?

a. Insults by friends are the greatest cause of anger for university students.

b. University students are likely to feel sad when they worry about getting a job after graduation.

c. University students are most likely to feel happy when they get good results on exams.

d. Material satisfaction is the greatest cause of happiness for university students.

Part III

Which statement is true of gender differences?

a. The assumption that males felt sad more often than females was not statistically supported.

b. Females are more likely to feel angry than males.

c. In all the emotions compared, there were significant differences between males and females.

d. The assumption that females felt happy more often than males was fully supported by a statistical comparison.

Useful Phrases

Choose appropriate words from the box to complete each sentence.

日本語に合うように下線部に入る語句を語群から組み合わせて選び、文を完成させましょう（語群では文頭に来る語も小文字で始めています）。

1. 「～ということがわかった」

_____ these changes were similar for Day 1 and Day 2.

2. 「他方では～」

_____, words and actions by friends and family were less frequently reported as causes of anger.

3. 「これはおそらく～ということが理由です」

_____ university students can spend more time on deepening friendships and have more opportunities to derive happiness from such affinity.

4. 「要約すれば」

_____, the study found that changes in emotions by hour were similar for Day 1 and Day 2.

> brief / this / the / that / on / it / other / found / hand / in /
> probably because / is / was

Summarize the Presentation

DL 106~110 · CD 2-36 ~ CD 2-40

Read the summary of the presentation and fill in the blanks to complete the sentences for each slide.

スライドを参考に、空所に適語を入れプレゼンテーションの要約を完成させましょう。

1.

Today's lecture:

Emotion of University Students in Daily Life

Today I'd like to talk to you about a study (¹   ) in 2000 that looked at emotions experienced by (²   ) (   ). There are three main sets of results that I would like to present today.

2.

Changes during 2 days

Day 1 ≒ Day 2

First, the study looked at (³   ) in emotion by hour during the two consecutive days, and found that these changes were (⁴   ) for Day 1 and Day 2, with peak and dip periods for anger and happiness being (⁵   ) between the two days.

3.

Group differences

University Students ≠ Junior High =

Next, the study (⁶   ) the causes of university students' emotions with those of (⁷   ) (   ) (   ) students. There were some (⁸   ) as well as some (⁹   ) between the two groups.

4. Gender differences

Finally, the comparison of males and females showed that there were some general (^{10}) trends. (^{11}) anger, males tended to feel anger (^{12}) (   ) than females. As for sadness, males tended to feel sad more often. As for happiness, females tended to feel happy more frequently than males.

5. Summary

• Changes in emotions were similar for Day 1 & Day 2

• Differences & similarities between Us & JHs

• Differing trends between males & females

In brief, the study found that changes in emotions by hour were similar for Day 1 and Day 2, with (^{13}) and dip periods for anger and happiness being consistent between the two days. In the (^{14}) (   ) junior high school students, some differences and similarities were found. In the (^{15}) comparison, there were no clear-cut differences between men and women, but there were some differing (^{16}).

プレゼンテーションのリハーサル

Presentation Tips

　プレゼンテーションの原稿やスライドができたら本番までに事前練習をしましょう。原稿を見ながら3回程度練習し、その後、原稿を見ずに（メモはＯＫ）3回程度練習しましょう。その際に、予定時間内で終わるかなども確認します。練習の際に、長すぎたり難しいと思った文は、短く簡潔にするとよいでしょう。また、スマホなどで自分の練習の様子を録音や録画して客観的に出来具合を確認してみてもよいです。個人練習ができたら、その後、機会があればクラスのグループなどでリハーサルを行って、出来の確認や改善点をあげてもらうとよいでしょう。個人やグループ練習の際には以下の項目に注意しましょう。事前練習をしっかりやれば、本番は自信をもって臨めるはずです。

【事前チェック】
□英語や内容はわかりやすいですか
□スライドはわかりやすいですか
□予定時間通りに終了していますか
□ジェスチャーやアイコンタクトをしていますか

▶️ Dictation and Shadowing

online / video

Step 1　Listen and complete the sentences with suitable words.　🎧 DL 111　💿 CD 2-41
音声を聞いて、空所に適切な語を入れましょう。

1. _____ _____ _____ _____ the presentation of the results, let us briefly look at the research method used in this study.

2. Now _____ _____ _____ _____ the three main sets of results.

3. _____ _____ _____ anger, university students more frequently reported actions, by other people and by themselves, as causes of anger.

4. _____ anger, males tended to feel anger more frequently than females.

Step 2　Following the video directions, practice A to D.
映像の指示にしたがって、A 〜 D の練習をしましょう。

A Say the sentences aloud for Step 1 with audio and text.
Step 1 の文を映像（テキストと音声）と一緒に発声しましょう。

B Say them aloud with the excerpted videos (with subtitles).
Step 1 の文を映像（字幕）と一緒に発声しましょう。

C Say them aloud with the excerpted videos (with only partially completed subtitles).
Step 1 の文を映像（一部以外はすべて空白の字幕）と
一緒に発声しましょう。

D Say them aloud with the excerpted videos (no subtitles).
Step 1 の文を映像（字幕なし）と一緒に発声しましょう。

顔の表情もバリエーション
豊かに発声してみましょう。

The Role of Criminal Jurisprudence

日本でも裁判員制度が導入されてしばらく経ちました。将来、裁判員の一人として法廷に立ち会い判決まで関与する可能性はゼロではありません。しかし法廷用語は何かしら難解な印象がありませんか？ このユニットでは、これからの刑法学の在り方について考えていきます。

Keywords Check

online audio
DL 112　CD 2-42

Choose the correct definition in Japanese for each word.
それぞれの単語の意味を選択肢から選びましょう。

1. jurisprudence	[　]	2. homicide	[　]
3. imprisonment	[　]	4. terminology	[　]
5. lay	[　]	6. self-defense	[　]
7. manslaughter	[　]	8. uphold	[　]
9. abdication	[　]	10. degenerate	[　]

a. 素人の・非専門家の　b. 過失致死罪　c. 〜を支持する　d. 投獄・懲役
e. 退化する　f. 正当防衛　g. 法律学　h. 専門用語　i. 放棄　j. 殺人罪・殺人行為

▶◀ Watch the Presentation (1st Viewing) online / video

Watch the presentation and answer T(true) or F(false) for each of the following sentences.

プレゼンテーション映像を通しで観て、次の文が正しければTを、そうでなければFを選びましょう。

1. Criminal theory in Japan is virtually all taken from German criminal code.

[T / F]

2. A lay judge system was introduced in Japan in 2019. [T / F]

3. People easily accept the verdict if it is decided based on social conventions.

[T / F]

4. The ultimate purpose of the law is to resolve actual incidents in line with common sense. [T / F]

▶◀ Focus for Better Understanding (2nd Viewing)

online / video online / audio

Watch three short parts of the presentation for a closer understanding and answer the questions.

次にプレゼンテーション映像をパートごとに観て、それぞれの問題に答えましょう。

Part I DL 113 CD 2-43

Why are legal terms difficult for average people to understand?

a. Because they are translated by professional translators, not by lay people.

b. Because they are expressed in German, which is one of the most difficult languages in the world.

c. Because they are translated from German or newly coined when no Japanese equivalents are found.

d. Because they are all taken from secret codes, not from everyday language.

Part II DL 114 CD 2-44

Which statement is NOT true of the case in question?

a. The man was hit by a train and lost his life.

b. The man was grasping the woman's coat sleeve.

c. The woman was persistently being harassed by the man on the platform.

d. The woman pushed the man off the platform to the train tracks on purpose.

Part III

Which of the following is true?

a. The man's surviving relatives would probably accept the verdict, which was based on common sense.

b. Everyone would accept those conclusions that are drawn from the theory based on adequate grounds.

c. The man's surviving relatives would think that he deserved death for what he did.

d. The woman's family would think that letting the man die was going a little too far.

Useful Phrases

Choose appropriate words from the box to complete each sentence.

日本語に合うように下線部に入る語句を語群から組み合わせて選び、文を完成させましょう（語群では文頭に来る語も小文字で始めています）。

1.「造り出すしかなかった」

The translators _____ a new word when there was no corresponding Japanese word.

2.「本末転倒」

This is completely _____.

3.「おそらく」

_____, we will feel torn between "this drunken man got what he deserved for harassing the woman," and "letting him die was going too far."

4.「〜にすぎない」

Basing such decisions on social convention itself is _____ abdication of responsibility.

> more / the cart / putting / than / than / choice / to create / no /
> before / but / had / more / likely / nothing / the horse

Summarize the Presentation

DL 116~120 · CD 2-46 ~ CD 2-50

Read the summary of the presentation and fill in the blanks to complete the sentences for each slide.

スライドを参考に、空所に適語を入れプレゼンテーションの要約を完成させましょう。

1.
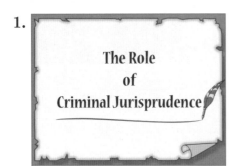

The Role
of
Criminal Jurisprudence

Today I am going to talk about the importance of legal theory. (^{1}) (   ), I'd like to discuss what we should do in order to (^{2}) (   ) it.

2.

Legal Terminology

Most of the legal terms have been translated from German

☞ difficult to understand

You may or may not know this, but criminal theory in Japan is (^{3}) all taken from (^{4}) criminal code theory. When translating legal terms, the translators had no choice but to create a new word. This led to (^{5}) (   ) which is out of touch with everyday language.

3.

Lay Judge System

introduced in Japan in May, 2009
♦ Criminal trials
   need to be reformed
   so as to be understood easily
   by lay judges

A (^{6}) (   ) (   ) was introduced in Japan in May 2009. Some say (^{7}) (   ) need to be reformed so that lay judges can easily understand what is going on in the courts. With regard to criminal theory as well, traditional legal courtroom debate is a (^{8}) (   ) (   ),

and the decision on whether or not an act is a criminal offense should be decided based on (^{9}) (   ).

4.

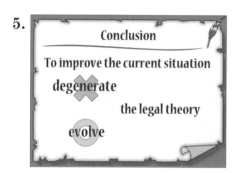

◆ Criminal theory

☞　The answer is

NO!!

Social convention is not
constantly & uniformly decided

Well, this is completely putting the cart before the horse. Complex debate is (¹⁰　　　　　　) if "social convention" is (¹¹　　　　　　) and (¹²　　　　　　) determined. However, "social convention" is not the same for all people at all times.

5.

Conclusion

To improve the current situation

degenerate

the legal theory

evolve

Naturally, the ultimate purpose of the law is to resolve actual incidents in line with common sense. The problem with the current situation is that the code can only be understood by (¹³　　　　　). The best way to improve this situation is not to allow the theory to "(¹⁴　　　　　)," but rather to have the theory "(¹⁵　　　　　)" to reach the

level at which it is possible to provide (¹⁶　　　　　　　) without using specialist terms.

質疑応答（1）オーディエンスの立場から

　　プレゼンテーションはプレゼンターとオーディエンスの双方がいて初めて成り立ちます。最低限１つは質問する心構えでプレゼンテーションを聞きましょう。発表内容に興味がある程、確かめたい点や疑問点が浮かんでくるものですが、通例発表の最後に質疑応答の時間が設けられていますので、その時に発言できるように質問内容をメモにまとめておきましょう。質疑応答の時間を独り占めしてしまわないように注意して、質問は明確かつ簡潔にし、質疑応答の場が、プレゼンターとオーディエンスの双方にとって建設的な場となるように心掛けましょう。
まずは以下のような表現を使った簡単な質問から始めてみましょう。

①自分の理解があいまいな場合

　I couldn't quite understand ~. Could you explain ~ again?

②もう一度、資料などを確かめたい場合

　Could you go back to the slide that shows ~?

③更なる情報を求める場合

　Could you give us another example of ~?

▶ Dictation and Shadowing

online/video

Step 1 Listen and complete the sentences with suitable words.   DL 121   CD 2-51
音声を聞いて、空所に適切な語を入れましょう。

1. This is probably one of the _____ _____ _____

_____ of the law.

2. This led to legal terminology which is _____ _____ _____

_____ everyday language.

3. _____ _____ the lay judge system is _____ _____,

criminal trials need to be reformed.

4. The _____ _____ of the law is to resolve actual incidents in

line with _____ _____.

Step 2 Following the video directions, practice A to D.
映像の指示にしたがって、A ～ D の練習をしましょう。

A Say the sentences aloud for Step 1 with audio and text.
Step 1 の文を映像（テキストと音声）と一緒に発声しましょう。

B Say them aloud with the excerpted videos (with subtitles).
Step 1 の文を映像（字幕）と一緒に発声しましょう。

C Say them aloud with the excerpted videos (with only partially completed subtitles).
Step 1 の文を映像（一部以外はすべて空白の字幕）と一緒に発声しましょう。

D Say them aloud with the excerpted videos (no subtitles).
Step 1 の文を映像（字幕なし）と一緒に発声しましょう。

顔の表情もバリエーション
豊かに発声してみましょう。

Diabetes: Symptoms and Prevention

糖尿病という病気をご存知でしょうか？ みなさんは自分には無縁と考えているかもしれません。糖尿病は現代人誰もがかかる恐れがあり、様々な合併症を生じる恐ろしい病気です。その原因と予防を考えてみましょう。

Keywords Check

online audio

Choose the correct definition in Japanese for each word.
それぞれの単語の意味を選択肢から選びましょう。

DL 122 CD 2-52

1. diabetes   [   ]   2. glucose   [   ]

3. metabolism   [   ]   4. pancreas   [   ]

5. duodenum   [   ]   6. autoimmune   [   ]

7. complications [   ]   8. nephropathy   [   ]

9. retinopathy   [   ]   10. neuropathy   [   ]

---

a. すい臓 **b.** ブドウ糖 **c.** 網膜症 **d.** 腎障害 **e.** 自己免疫の
f. 代謝 **g.** 合併症 **h.** 神経障害 **i.** 糖尿病 **j.** 十二指腸

▶ Watch the Presentation (1st Viewing) online / video

Watch the presentation and answer T(true) or F(false) for each of the following sentences.
プレゼンテーション映像を通しで観て、次の文が正しければ T を、そうでなければ F を選びましょう。

1. Egyptians found diabetes by observing insects. [T / F]

2. Insulin is one of many kinds of hormone that can lower the blood sugar level.

[T / F]

3. Patients with Type 1 diabetes lack insulin. [T / F]

4. The presenter didn't discussed prevention of diabetes. [T / F]

▶ Focus for Better Understanding (2nd Viewing)

online / video   online / audio

Watch three short parts of the presentation for a closer understanding and answer the questions.
次にプレゼンテーション映像をパートごとに観て、それぞれの問題に答えましょう。

Part I
🎧 DL 123 ⦿ CD 2-53

What is NOT mentioned as a typical early symptoms of diabetes?

a. constant headache

b. incurable thirst

c. frequent urination

d. blurred vision

Part II
🎧 DL 124 ⦿ CD 2-54

Where in the pancreas is insulin produced?

a. in the exocrine portion of the pancreas

b. in the endocrine portion of the pancreas

c. both in the exocrine and endocrine portions of the
pancreas

d. not in the pancreas

Part III

What causes Type 2 diabetes?

a. Type 1 diabetes

b. a viral infection

c. absolute lack of insulin

d. disorders of insulin receptors

Useful Phrases

Choose appropriate words from the box to complete each sentence.

日本語に合うように下線部に入る語句を語群から組み合わせて選び、文を完成させましょう（語群では文頭に来る語も小文字で始めています）。

1.「〜と密接に関連して」

Diabetes is _____ insulin production.

2.「〜の結果である」

Diabetes _____ a shortage of insulin.

3.「それゆえ〜にとどまる」

The cells stop processing glucose, _____

the bloodstream.

4.「私が前に述べたように」

Type 1 diabetes is difficult to treat because, _____,

it is an autoimmune disease.

> earlier / the result / as / linked to / remains in / which / closely /
>
> is / of / I / therefore / mentioned

Summarize the Presentation

DL 126~130   CD 2-56 ~ CD 2-60

Read the summary of the presentation and fill in the blanks to complete the sentences for each slide.

スライドを参考に、空所に適語を入れプレゼンテーションの要約を完成させましょう。

1.

DIABETES

Hello everyone and welcome. In my presentation today I am going to talk about (¹   ). First we'll look at the (²   ) of diabetes. Then we'll consider two types of diabetes and their (³   ). (⁴   ), we'll discuss ways to prevent diabetes.

2.

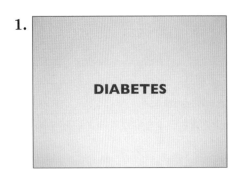

DIABETES AND INSULIN

· Insulin:
· Is a kind of hormone
· Lowers the blood sugar level
· Is produced by the pancreas

endocrine tissue

pancreas

islets of Langerhans

Typical early symptoms include pronounced (⁵   ), incurable thirst, more frequent urination, (⁶   ) vision and numbness in the legs, as well as (⁷   ) and red swelling in various parts of the body. Diabetes is closely linked to (⁸   ) production. Insulin is the only hormone that can (⁹   ) the concentration of glucose in the blood, also known as the blood sugar level.

3.

TWO TYPES OF DIABETES

Type I	Type 2
Absolute lack of insulin	Insulin is present; the receptors are not working
Autoimmune disease	Far more common

At present there are two main types of diabetes: Type 1 and Type 2. Type 1 diabetes is caused by an (¹⁰   ) lack of insulin. Type 1 diabetes is known as an (¹¹   ) disease. Type 2 diabetes is caused by a (¹²   ), rather than absolute, lack of insulin. This means that though insulin is present in the body, the insulin receptors are not reacting to the insulin, leading to insulin (¹³   ).

4.

INSULIN FUNCTIONS AND TOLERANCE

NORMAL insulin
glucose
insulin receptor
cell
energy

INSULIN TOLERANCE

When the body already has all the energy (^{14}) it needs, as in the case of obesity, the number of insulin receptors (^{15}), since the body does not require new proteins and lipids. In order to prevent potential damage to the liver and muscles caused by active oxygen associated with excess glucose conversion, the cells (^{16}) processing glucose, which therefore (^{17}) in the bloodstream.

5.

PREVENTION

· Avoid stress
· Avoid an excess intake of energy
· Exercise regularly to keep the muscles working

A healthy lifestyle can prevent diabetes!

Beyond 30 years of age, it is important to avoid (^{18}) and an excess intake of energy, and to keep the muscles working through (^{19}) exercise. This concludes today's presentation on the symptoms, forms and causes of diabetes. Diabetes can be prevented by maintaining a healthy (^{20}) lifestyle.

質疑応答（2）プレゼンターの立場から

Presentation Tips

　良いフィードバックを聞き手から受けることは大切ですが、質疑応答は質問に即座に的確に答えなくてはならず、発表者が最も緊張するのは、実は発表自体ではなく、発表後の質疑応答の時間かもしれません。限られた時間内で質疑応答は行われますので、質問しやすいようにわかりやすいプレゼンテーションやスライドを心がけましょう。

以下は覚えておくと役立つ表現です。

①質問がよく理解できない場合

　I'm afraid I didn't understand your question. Could you rephrase that more simply?

②即座に答えられない場合

　I'm afraid I don't know the answer right now. If you don't mind, I'd like to answer that question later.

③自分の答えが質問に答えられているか確認する場合

　Does that answer your question?

④考える時間が欲しい場合

　Let me see.

　発表は上手くできたのに、質疑応答になるとしどろもどろできちんと答えられないということがないように、予め想定問答で練習しておきましょう。

▶️ Dictation and Shadowing

online / video

Step 1　Listen and complete the sentences with suitable words.　🎧 DL 131　💿 CD 2-61
音声を聞いて、空所に適切な語を入れましょう。

1. _____ _____ _____, diabetes may appear to be a simple

   metabolic disorder related to sugars or carbohydrates.

2. If you notice any of these symptoms, you should see your local doctor to _____

   _____ _____ _____ _____.

3. Type 2 diabetes, on the other hand, is far more common, _____ _____

   _____ 90% of diabetes sufferers.

4. _____ _____ _____ _____ _____ the

   symptoms, forms and causes of diabetes.

Step 2　Following the video directions, practice A to D.
映像の指示にしたがって、A～Dの練習をしましょう。

A Say the sentences aloud for Step 1 with audio and text.
Step 1 の文を映像（テキストと音声）と一緒に発声しましょう。

B Say them aloud with the excerpted videos (with subtitles).
Step 1 の文を映像（字幕）と一緒に発声しましょう。

C Say them aloud with the excerpted videos (with only partially completed subtitles).
Step 1 の文を映像（一部以外はすべて空白の字幕）と
一緒に発声しましょう。

D Say them aloud with the excerpted videos (no subtitles).
Step 1 の文を映像（字幕なし）と一緒に発声しましょう。

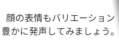

顔の表情もバリエーション
豊かに発声してみましょう。

Report on Ocean Noise: Natural Resources Defense Council

騒音公害は地上だけの問題と思っていませんか？ 実は今、広くて深い海の騒音が大きな問題となっています。人間の作り出した様々な音が海の生物の生存を脅かしているのです。私たちにできることは何か考えてみましょう。

Keywords Check

online / audio

Choose the correct definition in Japanese for each word.
それぞれの単語の意味を選択肢から選びましょう。

🎧 DL 132 ◎ CD 2-62

1. oceanographer   [   ]   2. proliferation   [   ]

3. mass stranding   [   ]   4. chronic   [   ]

5. rumble   [   ]   6. implement   [   ]

7. mitigation measure   [   ]   8. economies of scale   [   ]

9. reiterate   [   ]   10. devastating   [   ]

---

a. 軽減対策   **b.** 集団座礁   **c.** 蔓延   **d.** 海洋学者   **e.** 繰り返して言う
f. 慢性の   **g.** 壊滅的な   **h.** 実行する   **i.** 規模の経済性   **j.** ガラガラ鳴る音

▶️ Watch the Presentation (1st Viewing)

online video

Watch the presentation and answer T(true) or F(false) for each of the following sentences.
プレゼンテーション映像を通して観て、次の文が正しければ T を、そうでなければ F を選びましょう。

1. Divers and oceanographers often say that the ocean is a silent place. [T / F]

2. Hearing is probably the primary sense of whales, dolphins, and other marine species. [T / F]

3. There is no convincing evidence linking mass strandings to mid-frequency sonar. [T / F]

4. Action needs to be taken immediately to address the issue of ocean noise. [T / F]

▶️ Focus for Better Understanding (2nd Viewing)

online video   online audio

Watch three short parts of the presentation for a closer understanding and answer the questions.
次にプレゼンテーション映像をパートごとに観て、それぞれの問題に答えましょう。

Part I

DL 133   CD 2-63

Among the effects of ocean noise, which is supposed to have the most adverse impact on species like fin whales?

a. temporary hearing loss

b. the masking of biologically important sounds

c. a loss of sense of direction

d. chronic stress

Part II

DL 134   CD 2-64

Which of the following is NOT mentioned about the second leading contributors to ocean noise?

a. Seismic surveys are conducted to predict earthquakes.

b. Firing of air guns is intense enough to wash out whale calls.

c. High-energy seismic surveys are used to detect oil and gas deposits.

d. Seismic surveys are utilized by industry.

Part III

Which of the following is NOT included among the steps we should take?

a. to develop economies of scale

b. to hold global conferences annually

c. to commit to global and regional solutions

d. to implement a wider set of mitigation measures

Useful Phrases

Choose appropriate words from the box to complete each sentence.

日本語に合うように下線部に入る語句を語群から組み合わせて選び、文を完成させましょう（語群では文頭に来る語も小文字で始めています）。

1. 「〜において必要不可欠な役割を担う」

Sound _____ the lives of these marine creatures.

2. 「〜の現状」

What is _____ the problem of ocean noise?

3. 「〜の３つの主な要因」

There are _____ the problem of ocean noise that I would like to mention in particular.

4. 「警鐘」

The mass strandings that have emerged over the last several years are a _____ _____.

> state / leading / call / role / three / to / plays / the current / of /
> in / an essential / contributors / wake-up

Summarize the Presentation

online audio

DL 136~140 CD 2-66 ~ CD 2-70

Read the summary of the presentation and fill in the blanks to complete the sentences for each slide.

スライドを参考に、空所に適語を入れプレゼンテーションの要約を完成させましょう。

1.

NRDC's report

1. Present state
2. Leading contributors
3. Suggestions

I'd like to talk to you about the problem of ocean noise. Since 1999, the Natural Resources Defense Council, or NRDC (¹   ) (   ), has been investigating the effects of ocean noise on marine life. It has become (²   ) (   ) that the rise of ocean noise presents a significant, (³   )-(   ) (   ) to the marine environment.

2.

The present state

Some types of sound
kill
marine mammals

So, first of all, what is the (⁴   ) (   ) of the problem of ocean noise? Some types of sound are killing some species of (⁵   ) (   ). The acoustic environment is increasingly polluted by a variety of military, commercial, and (⁶   ) sources.

3.

Leading contributor 1

Military active sonar systems
Mid-frequency
⟹ whale strandings
Low-frequency
⟹ affect marine mammals

Now let us go on to look at the causes of this problem. There are three (⁷   ) (   ) to the problem of ocean noise that I would like to mention (⁸   ) (   ). Firstly, there are military active sonar systems. The second is high-energy seismic surveys. The third is perhaps the most obvious one for those of us up here above the waters — namely, ocean-going vessels, especially (⁹   ) (   ).

4.

Suggestions

1. **Wider mitigation measures**
2. **Economies of scale**
3. **Global & regional solutions**

Ocean noise is a significant environmental problem. But now is the moment when (^{10}) is possible. With this in mind, there are several steps that the NRDC recommends should be taken. Step one is to develop and implement a (^{11}) (   ) (   ) mitigation measures. Step two is to build economies of scale.

Finally, step three is to (^{12}) (   ) global and regional solutions.

5.

Summary

Marine life depends on sound

Human activities cause noises

➡ **Severe effects on marine life**

Act NOW before it's too late!

3 suggestions from NRDC

To wrap up, let me reiterate the main points I've made for you. Just as the (^{13}) (   ) (   ) depend heavily on sight in their daily lives, marine creatures rely very much on (^{14}). However, human activities are filling the oceans with (^{15}), and this is having sometimes (^{16})

(   ) on the inhabitants of the seas. Action needs to be taken to (^{17}) (   ) (   ) of ocean noise. And if we do not act now, it may be too late.

プレゼンテーションの Dos & Don'ts

Presentation Tips

Dos

☐ 発表を聞きに来る人はあなたに関心があります。まずちゃんと聴衆に向きあってから話を始めましょう。

☐ スライドの画面をめくるばかりでなく自分の言葉だけで伝える場面も含めましょう。

☐ 画面を読み上げたり指し示したりしなくても話が伝わるように準備しましょう。

☐ 口頭で説明する場合には何がトピックなのか途中でわかりにくくなりがちです。トピック→説明や例→再度トピックと繰り返すようにしましょう。

☐ 特に外国語で話す場合は早口になりがちです。ゆっくりとよどみなく話しましょう。

☐ 時間通りに始め時間通りに終わりましょう。話せなかった内容は質疑応答やセッションのあとで。

☐ 答えられない質問には、あとで連絡を取りましょうと答えればよいのです。答えられるものにしっかり答えましょう。

☐ 自信ある態度で始め、うまくいったという態度で終わりましょう。あなた自身をプレゼンテーションするのです。

Don'ts

☐ 原稿を読み上げていてはいけません。

☐ 謝りながら始め謝りながら終わってはいけません。

☐ 話し終わってホッとしてはいけません。次は質疑応答です。一番難しいのはここです。

◉◀ **Dictation and Shadowing**

online / video

Step 1 — Listen and complete the sentences with suitable words.
音声を聞いて、空所に適切な語を入れましょう。　🎧 DL 141　◉ CD 2-71

1. Finally, I'll make some suggestions _____ _____ _____

   might be done to reduce the impact of noise on the sea.

2. Now let us _____ _____ _____ _____

   _____ the causes of this problem.

3. _____ this _____ _____, there are several steps

   that the NRDC recommends should be taken.

4. I'd like to _____ _____ _____ _____ of my

   presentation today to outlining these steps.

Step 2 — Following the video directions, practice A to D.
映像の指示にしたがって、A ～ D の練習をしましょう。

A Say the sentences aloud for Step 1 with audio and text.
Step 1 の文を映像（テキストと音声）と一緒に発声しましょう。

B Say them aloud with the excerpted videos (with subtitles).
Step 1 の文を映像（字幕）と一緒に発声しましょう。

C Say them aloud with the excerpted videos (with only partially completed subtitles).
Step 1 の文を映像（一部以外はすべて空白の字幕）と一緒に発声しましょう。

D Say them aloud with the excerpted videos (no subtitles).
Step 1 の文を映像（字幕なし）と一緒に発声しましょう。

顔の表情もバリエーション
豊かに発声してみましょう。

プレゼンテーションで役立つ表現 124

プレゼンテーション本番はもちろん、日常会話やディスカッションでも役立つ表現を本編より厳選しました。

プレゼンテーションを開始する際の表現

例文と掲載ユニット

表現	例文と掲載ユニット
I will show you how to ~ (~の仕方を紹介します)	I will show you how to use familiar web search engines to find example sentences that are useful for learning English. (→ Introduction)
Thank you for the chance to ~ (~する機会をいただきありがとうございます)	Thank you for the chance to speak here today. (→ Unit 4)
I would like to talk to you about ~ (~についてお話ししたいと思います)	I would like to talk to you about stargazing. (→ Unit 4)
Today I will be describing ~ (本日は~を説明していきます)	Today I will be describing a technique for accurately determining the age of giant forest trees such as the *kiso hinoki* cypress. (→ Unit 5)
I'm here today to give ~ (本日は~を報告するために来ました)	I'm here today to give you some research findings regarding this longstanding mystery. (→ Unit 6)
present a speech on ~ (~に関する発表をする)	I'm here to present a speech on informal science education. (→ Unit 8)
This presentation will discuss ~ (本発表では~を議論します)	This presentation will discuss a way to provide young people with greater chances for learning science. (→ Unit 8)
I shall(will) try to ~ (~しようと思います)	In this presentation, I shall try to show some of the differences between sympathy and empathy within group relationships, ~ (→ Unit 9)
Let me begin my presentation by -ing (~することでプレゼンテーションを始めさせてください)	Let me begin my presentation by asking you a quick question. (→ Unit 10)
In my presentation today (本日のプレゼンテーションでは)	In my presentation today I am going to talk about diabetes. (→ Unit 13)
I am going to talk about ~ (~についてお話しします)	In my presentation today I am going to talk about diabetes. (→ Unit 13)
In this presentation, I'd like to present ~ (本発表では、~をお伝えします)	In this presentation, I'd like to present some of the findings. (→ Unit 14)

研究報告で使える表現

例文と掲載ユニット

表現	例文と掲載ユニット
be backed up by sufficient evidence (十分な証拠によって裏付けられる)	To make a strong argument, the reasons must be backed up by sufficient evidence. (→ Unit 1)
support your claims (主張を裏付けする)	Please work on using persuasive arguments to support your claims when writing essays. (→ Unit 1)
as reported in ~ (~で報告されているように)	It may be that the impact of parasitic mites and agricultural chemicals, as reported in the questionnaire and interview survey, has affected the ability of bees to fight off viruses and avoid disease. (→ Unit 2)
suggesting that ~ (そしてそのことは~ということを示唆している)	This conclusion is consistent with previous genetic research suggesting that bees are highly vulnerable to disease and the effects of pesticides. (→ Unit 2)

The same explanation also holds in the case of ~ (~の場合においても同じ説明が当てはまります)	The same explanation also holds in the case of figure skating. (→ Unit 3)
accurate date on ~ (~に関する正確なデータ)	We choose trees of known age and measure the carbon content of their growth rings to generate accurate data on actual Carbon 14 levels in each age range. (→ Unit 5)
take very precise measurements of ~ (~を非常に正確に測定する)	A team of scientists from Nagoya University used a particle accelerator to take very precise measurements of Carbon 14 concentrations. (→ Unit 5)
still have very little idea (まだよくわかっていない)	We still have very little idea of how exactly animals sense the seasons. (→ Unit 6)
We hope that this research will contribute to ~ (この研究が~に貢献することを願います)	We hope that this research will contribute to the advance of biology and to improving food production. (→ Unit 6)
have good enough data to disprove ~ (~を反証するのに十分なデータがある)	We did not have good enough data to disprove varied speculations about Mars and Martians. (→ Unit 7)
aim to ~ (~をすることを目指している)	We aim to enhance their interest in the natural sciences. (→ Unit 8)
draw a conclusion (結論を出す)	We can't immediately draw the same conclusion. (→ Unit 10)
get the same results (同じ結果を得る)	The researchers also carried out the same experiment on humans, using Nagoya University students, and got the same results. (→ Unit 10)
in order to figure out ~ (~を解明するために)	In order to figure out whether the fear observed is something instinctive or something learned, researchers used lab-reared monkeys that had never seen a snake. (→ Unit 10)
Previous studies show that ~ (先行研究では~ということが示されています)	Previous studies show that humans are quicker at detecting things that are frightening than things that are not. (→ Unit 10)
The results showed that ~ (その結果は~を示しました)	The results showed that when a photo of a snake was included among photos of flowers the monkeys were faster to choose than when a photo of flowers was shown among photos of snakes. (→ Unit 10)
What can we say from ~? (~から何が言えるでしょうか)	What can we say from the results of these experiments on reaction time? (→ Unit 10)
It was found that ~ (~ということが分かりました)	It was found that these changes were similar for Day 1 and Day 2. (→ Unit 11)
investigate the effects of ~ (~の影響を調査する)	The Natural Resources Defense Council has been investigating the effects of ocean noise on marine life. (→ Unit 14)
It has become increasingly clear that ~ (~ということが次第に明らかになってきています)	It has become increasingly clear that the rise of ocean noise presents a significant, long-term threat to the marine environment. (→ Unit 14)

話題・論点を提示する際の表現　　　　　　　　　　例文と掲載ユニット

I will clarify ~ (~を明らかにします)	In today's presentation, I will clarify what generally constitutes an argument. (→ Unit 1)
Now let us consider ~ (では~を考えてみましょう)	Now let us consider research into honeybee pathogen infection. (→ Unit 2)

We'll first look at ~ （まず初めに～をみてみます）	In this presentation, we'll first look at recent research in Japan and then try to determine the causes of this phenomenon. （→ Unit 2）
I'll look in detail at ~ （～を詳しく見て行きます）	In this presentation I'll look in detail at Lowell's main achievements. （→ Unit 7）
Now let us examine more closely ~ （では～をもっと詳細に検討してみましょう）	Now let us examine more closely what can be done to resolve the problems with the current situation. （→ Unit 8）
Now let us briefly look at ~ （さて～を少し見てみましょう）	Now let us briefly look at some background about today's Native Americans. （→ Unit 9）
We'll take a look together at ~ （～を一緒にみていきます）	We'll take a look together at some related research and think about this question. （→ Unit 10）
before moving on to ~ （～に移る前に）	Before moving on to the presentation of the results, let us briefly look at the research method used in this study. （→ Unit 11）
Now let us look in more detail at ~ （では～をもっと詳しく見てみましょう）	Now let us look in more detail at the causes of this problem. （→ Unit 14）

情報を追加・列挙する表現　　　　　　　　　例文と掲載ユニット

The first reason is ~, and the second is ~ （第一の理由は～て、第二の理由は～）	The first reason is that when the reading on the barometer drops it rains soon after, and the second is that the reading on the barometer is dropping fast. （→ Unit 1）
in addition to ~ （～に加えて）	In addition to honey production, bees also play an important role in the pollination of horticultural plants. （→ Unit 2）
firstly ~, secondly ~ （第一に～、第二に～）	In order to minimize the effect of light pollution, you need firstly to go as far away from big cities as possible and secondly to go as high in elevation as possible. （→ Unit 4）
moreover （その上）	Moreover, the fact that the metropolitan centers are relatively small helps minimize the level of light pollution. （→ Unit 4）
~ be divided into three parts （～を３つに分ける）	The presentation is divided into three parts. （→ Unit 8）
meaning that ~ （[前述を受けて] そしてそれは～を意味する）	However, this one-sided policy did not take into account the identity of the Native Americans, meaning that it did not permit smooth integration. （→ Unit 9）
first ~ , next ~ , finally ~ （初めに～、次に～、最後に～）	First, the study looked at changes in emotion... Next, the study compared the causes of university students' emotions with those of junior high school students... Finally, the comparison of males and females showed no clear-cut differences. （→ Unit 11）

例示するための表現　　　　　　　　　例文と掲載ユニット

specifically （具体的には）	Specifically, this will include phrase searches, site-specific searches and, finally, wildcard searches. （→ Introduction）
Let's say that ~ （例えば～だとしてみましょう）	Let's say that you wrote a self-introduction. （→ Introduction）
Here is a graphic illustration of ~ （ここに～の図解があります）	Here is a graphic illustration of argument (c). （→ Unit 1）

The list goes on and on. （まだまだ例はたくさんあります）	The list goes on and on. (→ Unit 4)
~ and so forth （～など）	Temperature and rainfall also fluctuate with the seasons, but they are not the most reliable factors, with some winters being warmer and some summers being cooler than usual, and the rainy season sometimes turning out dry, and so forth. (→ Unit 6)
give a simple explanation of ~ （～について簡単な説明をする）	In this presentation, I've given a simple explanation of how the seasons trigger changes in physiological functions of certain creatures. (→ Unit 6)
for instance （例えば）	Lafcadio Hearn, for instance, cited Lowell's The Soul of the Far East as an inspiration for his decision to visit Japan. (→ Unit 7)
as you can see here （ここにご覧のように）	As you can see here, the monkeys were shown a number of photos of snakes and flowers on a computer screen, ~ (→ Unit 10)
Let me give you an example. （1 つ例を挙げてみましょう）	Let me give you an example based on an actual case ruling by the Chiba District Court on September 17, 1987. (→ Unit 12)
as in the case of ~ （～の場合のように）	When the body already has all the energy reserves it needs, as in the case of obesity, the number of insulin receptors decreases. (→ Unit 13)
such as ~ （［例えば］～などの）	Other sources of noise, such as the air guns used in seismic surveys, may have similar effects. (→ Unit 14)

言いかえ表現　　　　　　　　　　　　　　　　　　例文と掲載ユニット

put simply （簡潔に言うと）	Put simply, whether or not an argument is persuasive depends on whether or not the reasons for the argument are reliable. (→ Unit 1)
in other words （言いかえれば）	In other words, the virus infection rates seem to differ from one beekeeper to the next. (→ Unit 2)
in technical terms （専門用語で言うと）	Physics shows that the rotation strength, the "angular momentum" in technical terms, is determined by the speed of rotation and the moment of inertia. (→ Unit 3)
to put it another way （言い換えれば）	To put it another way, in many countries, young people are losing interest in science learning. (→ Unit 8)
The bottom line is that ~ （要するに～、つまるところは～）	So the bottom line is that something needs to be done to move away from the current traditional, outdated curriculum. (→ Unit 8)
for short （略して）	I have set up the Permanent European Resource Center for Informal Learning, or "PENCIL" for short. (→ Unit 8)
so-called ~ （いわゆる～、～と言われる）	However in the second half of the 19th century, the United States attempted to civilize the so-called "pathetic" Indians by bringing them Christianity and education. (→ Unit 9)
in brief （要約すれば）	In brief, the study found that changes in emotions by hour were similar for Day 1 and Day 2. (→ Unit 11)
namely （すなわち）	The third leading contributor is perhaps the most obvious one for those of us up here above the waters – namely, ocean-going vessels. (→ Unit 14)

原因・結果・理由を述べる表現 例文と掲載ユニット

determine the causes of ~ （～の原因を突き止める）	In this presentation, we'll first look at recent research in Japan and then try to determine the causes of this phenomenon. (→ Unit 2)
be caused by ~ （～によって引き起こされる）	The survey found that the drop in the bee population was caused by parasitic mites as well as the impact of agricultural chemicals used by farmers. (→ Unit 2)
as a result（結果として）	But although bees may be infected, they do not necessarily develop diseases as a result. (→ Unit 2)
There is another factor in ~ （～において他の要因があります）	There is another factor in successfully performing a multiple-rotation jump, namely the height of the jump. (→ Unit 3)
That is why ~（それが理由で～、だから～）	Midori Ito was not only small, she also had excellent jumping ability, and that is why she was able to perform the triple Axel. (→ Unit 3)
You cannot ~ just because ... （ただ…というだけでは～できません）	~ you cannot succeed as an athlete just because you are large or small. (→ Unit 3)
accordingly（結果として）	Birds reduce their body weight as much as possible to enable flight, and accordingly adjust the size of their sexual organs in line with the breeding season. (→ Unit 6)
A lead to B（A が B をもたらす）	... but the search for Pluto led to the thorough observation of the furthest areas of our solar system. (→ Unit 7)
consequently（それ故に）	This led to legal terminology which is out of touch with everyday language, and consequently difficult for the average person to understand. (→ Unit 12)
be the result of ~（～の結果である）	Diabetes is the result of a shortage of insulin. (→ Unit 13)
... which therefore ~ （…そしてその結果～）	~ the cells stop processing glucose, which therefore remains in the bloodstream. (→ Unit 13)

問題解決に関する表現 例文と掲載ユニット

beyond the scope of ~ （～の手に負えない）	The solution to this problem is beyond the scope of beekeepers alone. (→ Unit 2)
in order to find ways to ~ （～する方法を見つけるために）	It requires a coordinated effort from farmers and beekeepers in order to find ways to improve the health of bees and restore the bee population to its proper level. (→ Unit 2)
outline a specific solution （具体的な解決策の概要を述べる）	Then, in the third part I will outline my specific solution. (→ Unit 8)
The best way to improve this situation is ~ （この状況を改善する最善の方法は～です）	The best way to improve this situation is not to allow the theory to "degenerate," but rather to have the theory "evolve"~ (→ Unit 12)
The issue here is that ~ （ここで問題なのは～です）	However, the issue here is that what we call "social convention" is not the same for all people at all times. (→ Unit 12)
The problem with ~ is that ... （～の問題点は…です）	The problem with the current situation is that the code can only be understood by specialists. (→ Unit 12)
address a problem（問題に対処する）	How necessary or urgent is it, to address the problem of ocean noise? (→ Unit 14)
implement measures（対策を講じる）	Step one is to develop and implement a wider set of mitigation measures. (→ Unit 14)

make some suggestions as to ~ （～に関して提言をする）	I'll make some suggestions as to what might be done to reduce the impact of noise on the sea. (→ Unit 14)

類似・相違・対比を表す表現　　　　　　　　　　例文と掲載ユニット

and vice versa （逆の場合も同じ）	In other words, when the rotation strength is fixed, the smaller the moment of inertia, the faster the speed of rotation, and vice versa. (→ Unit 3)
compared to ~ （～と比較すると）	It is not surprising that you get different sets of interesting celestial objects to observe because you are looking in different directions at the sky compared to when you are observing from the northern hemisphere. (→ Unit 4)
meanwhile （一方では）	Meanwhile, living trees exchange air and carbon on a continuous basis. (→ Unit 5)
in contrast （それに比べ）	In contrast, Noto is a refreshing read even today. (→ Unit 7)
similarly to ~ （～と同様に）	For happiness, similarly to junior high school students, physiological satisfaction, achievement and affinity were major causes among the university student subjects. (→ Unit 11)
There is a difference between ~ （～の間には違いがあります）	But there was a difference between the two groups. (→ Unit 11)
just as ~ （～とまったく同じように）	Just as the majority of humans depend heavily on sight in their daily lives, marine creatures rely very much on sound. (→ Unit 14)

推測・仮定・断定をする表現　　　　　　　　　　例文と掲載ユニット

be likely to ~ （～する可能性がある）	We have seen that the cause is likely to be a chain of factors. (→ Unit 2)
without a doubt （疑いなく）	One of the reasons is their belief that "Science is difficult." However, without a doubt, there is no room for any society to miss the train of scientific innovation. (→ Unit 8)
It is true that ~ （～ということは事実です）	On the other hand, it is true that there are differences worldwide in the way young people look at science. (→ Unit 8)
It is assumed that ~ （～と推測されます）	~ it is assumed that, as part of the evolutionary process, our ancestors developed pathways in the brain for processing visually-received information, to help them survive. (→ Unit 10)
One reasonable assumption is that ~ （1 つの合理的推測は～です）	However, one reasonable assumption is that the ability of humans to pick out snakes has a common root with the innate ability of monkeys to quickly detect snakes. (→ Unit 10)
You may or may not know this, but ~ （ご存知かどうかわかりませんが、～）	You may or may not know this, but criminal theory in Japan is virtually all taken from German criminal code theory. (→ Unit 12)
more than likely （恐らく）	More than likely, we will feel torn between "this drunken man got what he deserved for harassing the woman," and "letting him die was going too far." (→ Unit 12)
fully aware that ~ （～を十分に認識している）	~ we will be fully aware that neither argument is lacking in common sense. (→ Unit 12)
at first glance （一見したところ）	At first glance diabetes may appear to be a simple metabolic disorder ~ (→ Unit 13)

強調をする表現　　　　　　　　　　　　　　　　　　　例文と掲載ユニット

The important point here is ~ （ここで重要なのは~です）	The important point here is to always check the context of the expressions you find. (→ Introduction)
Note that ~ （~ということ留意してください）	Note that there may be some search engines with which these methods do not work. (→ Introduction)
I repeat. （繰り返します）	I repeat, what is an argument? (→ Unit 1)
let alone ~ （~は言うまでもなく）	This is because they are much fainter than planets like Venus and Jupiter, let alone the much brighter Moon, ~ (→ Unit 4)
It is not surprising that ~ （~というのは当然のことです）	It is not surprising that you get different sets of interesting celestial objects to observe ~ (→ Unit 4)
Our top priority is to ~ （私たちの第一の目的は~することです）	Thus our top priority is to turn around students' belief. (→ Unit 8)
be far from ~ （全く~ない）	Science education is far from attracting crowds ~ (→ Unit 8)
in any case （いずれにしても）	But in any case, countries that have taken the risk of shaking up the science curriculum seem to have better results than others which have not taken this risk. (→ Unit 8)
nothing more than ~ （~にすぎない）	Basing such decisions on social convention itself is nothing more than abdication of responsibility. (→ Unit 12)
no longer a matter of ~ （もはや~の問題ではない）	This is no longer a matter of serious debate. (→ Unit 14)

プレゼンテーションを締めくくる際の表現　　　　　　　例文と掲載ユニット

In this presentation we have examined ~ （この発表では、~を検証してきました）	In this presentation we have examined recent research into the bee population in Japan ~ (→ Unit 2)
I'm afraid that's all the time we have now. （そろそろ時間となりました）	I'm afraid that's all the time we have now. (→ Unit 8)
Let me summarize ~ （~の要点を述べます）	So, to wrap up, let me summarize the main points of my talk. (→ Unit 8)
Thank you very much for your attention. （ご清聴ありがとうございました）	Thank you very much for your attention. (→ Unit 8)
It is time to move on to the conclusion. （そろそろまとめの時間となりました）	Well, now it is time to move on to the conclusion. (→ Unit 10)
Let us conclude by -ing （~をして発表の結びとします）	So, let us conclude by summarizing the findings of the study. (→ Unit 11)
Thank you for your time today. （お時間ありがとうございました）	Thank you for your time today. (→ Unit 13)
devote the final part of my presentation to ~ （発表の最後のパートを~に充てる）	I'd like to devote the final part of my presentation today to outlining these steps. (→ Unit 14)
That concludes ~ （これで~を終わります）	Well, that concludes the body of my presentation. (→ Unit 14)
to wrap up （締めくくりに）	To wrap up, let me reiterate the main points I've made for you. (→ Unit 14)

このテキストのメインページ
www.kinsei-do.co.jp/plusmedia/40⁹

次のページの QR コードを読み取ると
直接ページにジャンプできます

オンライン映像配信サービス「plus⁺Media」について

本テキストの映像と音声は plus⁺Media ページ（www.kinsei-do.co.jp/plusmedia）から、ストリーミング再生でご利用いただけます。手順は以下に従ってください。

ログイン

● ご利用には、ログインが必要です。
　サイトのログインページ（www.kinsei-do.co.jp/plusmedia/login）へ行き、plus⁺Media パスワード（次のページのシールをはがしたあとに印字されている数字とアルファベット）を入力します。

● パスワードは各テキストにつき１つです。
　有効期限は、はじめてログインした時点から１年間になります。

ログインページ

[利用方法]

次のページにある QR コード、もしくは plus⁺Media トップページ（www.kinsei-do.co.jp/plusmedia）から該当するテキストを選んで、そのテキストのメインページにジャンプしてください。

plus+Media トップ　　　　メインページ

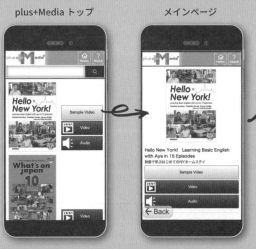

メニューページ　　　　　再生画面

「Video」「Audio」をタッチすると、それぞれのメニューページにジャンプしますので、そこから該当する項目を選べば、ストリーミングが開始されます。

[推奨環境]

iOS (iPhone, iPad)	OS: iOS 6 〜 13 ブラウザ：標準ブラウザ	Android	OS: Android 4.x 〜 9.0 ブラウザ：標準ブラウザ、Chrome
PC	OS: Windows 7/8/8.1/10, MacOS X　ブラウザ: Internet Explorer 10/11, Microsoft Edge, Firefox 48以降, Chrome 53以降, Safari		

※最新の推奨環境についてはウェブサイトをご確認ください。
※上記の推奨環境を満たしている場合でも、機種によってはご利用いただけない場合もあります。また、推奨環境は技術動向等により変更される場合があります。予めご了承ください。

このシールをはがすと
plus+Media 利用のための
パスワードが
記載されています。

一度はがすと元に戻すことは
できませんのでご注意下さい。

◀ ここからはがして下さい

4099 College
Presentation

plus+Media

本書にはCD（別売）があります

College Presentation
Bridge to Better Communication
プレゼンテーションを観て学ぶ 英語コミュニケーション

2020 年 1 月 20 日 初版第 1 刷発行
2022 年 3 月 31 日 初版第 4 刷発行

編　者　英語プレゼンテーション
　　　　教材開発研究チーム

発行者　福　岡　正　人
発行所　株式会社　金星堂

（〒101-0051）東京都千代田区神田神保町 3-21
Tel. (03) 3263-3828 (営業部)
(03) 3263-3997 (編集部)
Fax (03) 3263-0716
http://www.kinsei-do.co.jp

編集担当　長島吉成　　　　　　　　　　　　　　Printed in Japan
印刷所・製本所／倉敷印刷株式会社

ISBN978-4-7647-4099-0　C1082